Standardized Test Tutor

Test Tutor

MATH

Practice Tests With Problem-by-Problem Strategies and Tips That Help Students Build Test-Taking Skills and Boost Their Scores

SCHOLASTIC

GRADE **6**

Michael Priestley

Scholastic Inc. grants teachers permission to photocopy the reproducible pages from this mini-book
for classroom use. No other part of this publication may be reproduced in whole or in part, or stored in
a retrieval system, or transmitted in any form or by any means, electronic, mechanical, photocopying,
recording, or otherwise, without written permission of the publisher. For information regarding permission,
write to Scholastic Inc., 557 Broadway, New York, NY 10012.

Editor: Maria L. Chang
Cover design by Brian LaRossa
Interior design by Creative Pages, Inc.
Illustrations by Creative Pages, Inc.

ISBN-13: 978-0-545-09608-9
ISBN-10: 0-545-09608-1
Copyright © 2009 by Michael Priestley
Printed in the U.S.A.

1   2   3   4   5   6   7   8   9   10   40   15 14 13 12 11 10 09

Contents

Welcome to *Test Tutor!*

Students in schools today take a lot of tests, especially in reading and math. Some students naturally perform well on tests, and some do not. But just about everyone can get better at taking tests by learning more about what's on the test and how to answer the questions. How many students do you know who could benefit from working with a tutor? How many would love to have someone sit beside them and help them work their way through the tests they have to take?

That's where *Test Tutor* comes in. The main purpose of *Test Tutor* is to help students learn what they need to know in order to do better on tests. Along the way, *Test Tutor* will help students feel more confident as they come to understand the content and learn some of the secrets of success for multiple-choice tests.

The Test Tutor series includes books for reading and books for math in a range of grades. Each *Test Tutor* book in mathematics has three full-length practice tests designed specifically to resemble the state tests that students take each year. The math skills measured on these practice tests have been selected from an analysis of the skills tested in ten major states, and the questions have been written to match the multiple-choice format used in most states.

The most important feature of this book is the friendly Test Tutor. He will help students work through the tests and achieve the kind of success they are looking for. This program is designed so that students may work through the tests independently by reading the Test Tutor's helpful hints. Or you may work with the student as a tutor yourself, helping him or her understand each problem and test-taking strategy along the way. You can do this most effectively by following the Test Tutor's guidelines included in the pages of this book.

Three Different Tests

There are three practice tests in this book: Test 1, Test 2, and Test 3. Each test has 54 multiple-choice items with four answer choices (A, B, C, D). All three tests measure the same skills in almost the same order, but they provide different levels of tutoring help.

Test 1 provides step-by-step guidance to help students work through each problem, as in the sample on the next page. The tips in Test 1 are detailed and thorough, and they are written specifically for each math item to help students figure out how to solve the problem.

Sample 1

In Canada, the average life expectancy is 76.9 years for men and 83.7 years for women. On average, how much longer do women live than men?

Ⓐ 3.2 years

Ⓑ 6.8 years

Ⓒ 7.8 years

Ⓓ 160.6 years

To find how much longer women live than men, subtract the average age for men from the average for women.

Test 2 provides a test-taking tip for each item, as in the sample below, but the tips are less detailed than in Test 1. These tips help guide the student toward the solution to each problem without giving away too much. Students must take a little more initiative.

Sample 2

At the Olympics in 1896, the winner of the men's high jump cleared 1.81 meters. In 2004, the winner cleared 2.63 meters. How much higher did the winner jump in 2004?

Ⓐ 0.02 m

Ⓑ 0.21 m

Ⓒ 0.72 m

Ⓓ 0.82 m

Look for key words to help you understand the question.

Test 3 does not provide test-taking tips. It assesses the progress students have made. After working through Tests 1 and 2 with the help of the Test Tutor, students should be more than ready to score well on Test 3 without too much assistance. Success on this test will help students feel confident and prepared for taking real tests.

Other Helpful Features

In addition to the tests, this book provides some other helpful features. First, on page 64, you will find an **answer sheet**. When students take the tests, they may mark their answers by filling in bubbles directly on the test pages, or they may mark their answers on a copy of the answer sheet instead, as they will be required to do in most standardized tests. You may want to have students mark their answers on the test pages for Test 1, and then use an answer sheet for Tests 2 and 3 to help them get used to filling in bubbles.

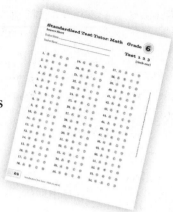

Second, beginning on page 65, you will find a detailed **answer key** for each test. The answer key lists the correct response and explains how to solve the problem. It also identifies the skill tested by each question, as in the sample below.

Answer Key for Sample 1

Correct response: **B**
(*Add, subtract, multiply, and divide decimals*)
To find the difference in life expectancies, subtract the men's average (76.9 years) from the women's average (83.7 years): $83.7 - 76.9 = 6.8$ years.

Incorrect choices:

A reflects an error in subtracting $76.9 - 83.7$ using only the last two digits.

C is the result of a computation error in subtracting $83.7 - 76.9$ as the student fails to "borrow" a one from 83.

D is the result of adding $83.7 + 76.9$ instead of subtracting.

As the sample indicates, this question measures the sudent's ability to add, subtract, multiply, and divide decimals. This information can help you determine which skills the student has mastered and which ones still cause difficulty.

Finally, the answer key explains why each incorrect answer choice, or "distractor," is incorrect. This explanation can help reveal what error the student might have made. For example, one distractor in an addition problem might be the result of subtracting two numbers instead of adding them together. Knowing this could help the student understand that he or she used the wrong operation.

At the back of this book, you will find two scoring charts. The **Student Scoring Chart** can help you keep track of each student's scores on all three tests and in different subtests, such as "Number and Number Sense" or "Measurement and Geometry." The **Classroom Scoring Chart** can be used to record the scores for all students on all three tests. This will help illustrate how much progress students have made from Test 1 to Test 3. Ideally, students should score higher on each test as they go through them. However, keep in mind that students get a lot of tutoring help on Test 1, some help on Test 2, and no help on Test 3. So if a student's scores on all three tests are fairly similar, that could still be a very positive sign that the student is better able to solve problems independently and will achieve even greater success on future tests.

Test Tutor says:

Directions: Read each question. Look at the Test Tutor's tip for answering the question. Then find the answer. You may do your work on this page or on scrap paper. Mark your answer by filling in the correct bubble.

1. Which answer lists the numbers in order from least to greatest?

   Ⓐ $0.3, \frac{5}{20}, \frac{7}{5}, 1$

   Ⓑ $\frac{5}{20}, 0.3, \frac{7}{5}, 1$

   Ⓒ $0.3, \frac{5}{20}, 1, \frac{7}{5}$

   Ⓓ $\frac{5}{20}, 0.3, 1, \frac{7}{5}$

> To compare and order these numbers, convert all of the numbers to decimals or to fractions with a common denominator.

2. The Big M store is having a sale. The chart below shows the sale discounts.

The Big M Clothing Sale!		
Item	Original Price	Discount
Jeans	$45	10%
Sweater	$50	20%
Shoes	$60	40%
Jacket	$80	50%

Which item costs the least during the sale?

   Ⓐ jeans

   Ⓑ sweater

   Ⓒ shoes

   Ⓓ jacket

> To compare the sale prices for these items, first apply the discount to the original price of each item. For example, the sale price for jeans is $45 minus a discount of 10% of $45.

3. Which integers are in order from least to greatest?

   Ⓐ $-6, -3, 1, 2$

   Ⓑ $2, 0, -3, -5$

   Ⓒ $-3, 4, -6, 8$

   Ⓓ $-4, -5, -7, -9$

> Remember that a negative integer (such as −5) has less value than a positive integer (such as 5). Watch for the negative signs as you order the numbers.

Test Tutor says:

4. In one year, an airplane flew 534,726 miles. Which digit in this number is in the ten thousands place?

(A) 3

(B) 4

(C) 5

(D) 7

> To find place value, read the number 534,726 aloud and write it in expanded form. For example, the digit 2 stands for 20.

5. What is the prime factorization of 56?

(A) 8×7

(B) $2 \times 4 \times 7$

(C) $2 \times 2 \times 2 \times 2 \times 7$

(D) $2^3 \times 7$

> A prime number has only two factors, the number itself and 1. Start with any two factors that equal 56, then break down any composite (non-prime) numbers.

6. A total of 24 teachers, 48 parents, and 304 students go on a field trip. The principal wants to divide everyone into smaller groups. If the teachers, parents, and students are all divided equally among the groups, what is the greatest number of groups the principal can create?

(A) 4

(B) 8

(C) 12

(D) 24

> To find the greatest number of groups, you must find the greatest common factor of 24, 48, and 304.

7. The diameter of the planet Saturn is about 120,000 kilometers. How should this number be written in scientific notation?

(A) 12×10^4

(B) 1.2×10^4

(C) 1.2×10^5

(D) 1.2×10^6

> A number written in scientific notation is found by multiplying a number by a power of 10. The number has one digit to the left of the decimal point, and the power of 10 shows how many places the decimal point was moved.

Test Tutor says:

8. The chart below shows the numbers of campers and counselors at Sunny Acres Summer Camp for its first 4 years.

	Year 1	Year 2	Year 3	Year 4
Campers	18	30	36	42
Counselors	3	5	6	7

What is the ratio of campers to counselors?

Ⓐ 6 to 1

Ⓑ 3 to 5

Ⓒ 5 to 6

Ⓓ 18 to 7

> To find the ratio, compare the number of campers to counselors each year in the form of a fraction in lowest terms.

9. A theater sells $5,904 worth of tickets for a show. If tickets cost $12 each, how many tickets did the theater sell?

Ⓐ 492

Ⓑ 889

Ⓒ 5,916

Ⓓ 70,848

> To find the number of tickets sold, divide the total cost of the tickets by the cost of one ticket.

10. A developer buys two plots of land. One is $3\frac{2}{3}$ acres and the other is $2\frac{1}{6}$ acres. How many acres of land does the developer buy all together?

Ⓐ $5\frac{1}{2}$

Ⓑ $5\frac{5}{6}$

Ⓒ 6

Ⓓ $7\frac{17}{18}$

> To find the total number of acres, add the number of acres in each plot. Use a common denominator of 6.

11. In a race, the winner finished in 46.69 seconds. The second-place runner finished in 48.21 seconds. What was the difference between the first- and second-place times?

Ⓐ 1.52 seconds   Ⓒ 2.62 seconds

Ⓑ 2.48 seconds   Ⓓ 2.90 seconds

> To find the difference between first and second place, subtract one time from the other.

Standardized Test Tutor: Math (Grade 6) © 2009 by Michael Priestley, Scholastic Teaching Resources

Test Tutor says:

12. Trina made this scale drawing of her house.

If the height of the house is 28 feet, how wide is it?

Ⓐ 21 ft

Ⓑ 22 ft

Ⓒ 24 ft

Ⓓ 42 ft

> Look at the drawing to find the height of the house in units. Find the scale used (1 unit = ? feet). Then apply the scale to find the width in feet.

13. On Monday, the low temperature for the day was 10°F. On Friday, the low temperature was −4°F. How much colder was the temperature on Friday than on Monday?

Ⓐ 4°F   Ⓒ 10°F

Ⓑ 6°F   Ⓓ 14°F

> To find the difference in temperature, subtract one temperature from the other. Remember, $a - (-b) = a + b$.

14. Dexter buys 2.98 pounds of potatoes at $1.59 per pound. Which is the best estimate of how much the potatoes cost?

Ⓐ $4.50   Ⓒ $4.80

Ⓑ $4.60   Ⓓ $6.00

> Round the weight to the nearest pound and the price to an easier number to work with, then multiply.

15. Evaluate $6 + 4(8 − 4) \div 2$ using order of operations.

Ⓐ 10

Ⓑ 11

Ⓒ 14

Ⓓ 20

> Follow the order of operations (PEMDAS) to solve this problem: Parentheses first, then multiplication and division from left to right, and finally addition and subtraction from left to right.

16. When added together, Matt and Selena's weights equal 187 pounds. If Selena's weight is 85, which equation could be used to find Matt's weight, (M)?

Ⓐ $187 - 85 = M$

Ⓑ $187 + 85 = M$

Ⓒ $M - 85 = 187$

Ⓓ $M \times 85 = 187$

> Write a number sentence that expresses the problem. Match your number sentence with one of the answer choices.

17. In Amelia's freezer, she has 1 gallon of coffee ice cream. At her picnic, she and her friends ate $\frac{2}{3}$ of the gallon. The next day, she and her parents ate another $\frac{1}{6}$ of the gallon. Then her grandmother gave them $\frac{1}{2}$ gallon of strawberry ice cream. How much ice cream does Amelia's family have now?

Ⓐ $\frac{1}{3}$ gallon   Ⓒ 1 gallon

Ⓑ $\frac{2}{3}$ gallon   Ⓓ $1\frac{1}{3}$ gallons

> Write a number sentence to solve this problem. Use a common denominator of 6. Pay attention to the language used so you know whether to add or subtract.

18. A boat starts at Canton and travels 140 miles downriver to Sandy Plain. It stops to drop off some cargo and then continues another 30 miles down the river to Rocky Point. At Rocky Point, the ship turns around and travels 90 miles back up the river to Deerfield. How far is Deerfield from Canton?

> Label the diagram with the distances if that will help you. Use the diagram to help you write a number sentence for this problem.

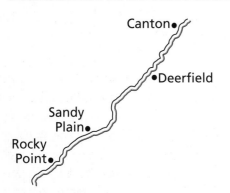

Ⓐ 20 miles   Ⓒ 80 miles

Ⓑ 50 miles   Ⓓ 260 miles

19. A tree is 1.6 meters tall. How many centimeters tall is it?

Ⓐ 16 cm   Ⓒ 1,600 cm

Ⓑ 160 cm   Ⓓ 16,000 cm

> Keep in mind that 1 meter = 100 centimeters.

20. Rahul is putting a fence around his square garden. Each side of the garden is $15\frac{5}{6}$ feet long. About how much fencing does Rahul need to buy?

Ⓐ 60 ft

Ⓑ 64 ft

Ⓒ 225 ft

Ⓓ 256 ft

> Notice the word *about* in the question. That means round to the nearest foot.

21. A triangular courtyard has a perimeter of 90 feet. If two of the sides measure 25 feet each, how long is the third side?

Ⓐ 7.2 ft

Ⓑ 25 ft

Ⓒ 40 ft

Ⓓ 65 ft

> The perimeter of the triangle is the sum of its three sides.

22. Ahmed is painting the entire outside of the rectangular box shown below.

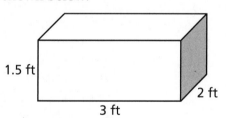

1.5 ft   3 ft   2 ft

What is the total surface area that he will paint?

Ⓐ 9 sq ft

Ⓑ 13.5 sq ft

Ⓒ 21 sq ft

Ⓓ 27 sq ft

> To find the surface area of the box, find the area of every side. Remember that a box has six sides. Pay attention to each side's measurement.

23. Toni puts a circular kiddie pool in the backyard for her little brother. If the diameter of the kiddie pool is 8 feet, what is the area that the pool will cover?

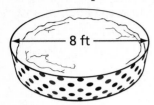

Ⓐ 4π sq ft   Ⓒ 16π sq ft

Ⓑ 8π sq ft   Ⓓ 64π sq ft

> The formula for the area of a circle is $A = \pi r^2$. The radius (r) of a circle is half the diameter.

24. What is the sum of the interior angles in a pentagon?

Ⓐ 540°

Ⓑ 720°

Ⓒ 900°

Ⓓ 1260°

> Remember that a three-sided figure has 180° and for each additional side you add another 180°. A pentagon has five sides.

25. Estimate the measure of ∠ABC.

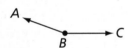

Ⓐ 80°   Ⓒ 130°

Ⓑ 110°   Ⓓ 160°

> Compare this angle to a right angle (90°) and a straight angle (180°).

26. Which angle below is an acute angle?

> Remember that an acute angle is less than 90°.

Standardized Test Tutor: Math (Grade 6) © 2009 by Michael Priestley, Scholastic Teaching Resources

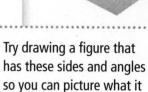

27. Andrew draws a polygon that has four equal sides, two acute angles, and two obtuse angles. What shape has he drawn?

Ⓐ parallelogram

Ⓑ square

Ⓒ rectangle

Ⓓ trapezoid

> Try drawing a figure that has these sides and angles so you can picture what it looks like.

28. The figure below is a rectangle.

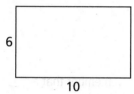

Which polygon is similar to the rectangle above?

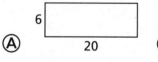

> Look for another shape with the same length-to-width ratio as the rectangle shown.

29. Julio gets a package in the mail that has one square side and four triangular sides. What is the shape of the package?

Ⓐ rectangular prism

Ⓑ triangular prism

Ⓒ triangular pyramid

Ⓓ square pyramid

> Sketch the figure described so you can picture it. Remember, a pyramid has one base and a prism has two.

30. Natalie puts her pencil down on point *A* in the coordinate grid.

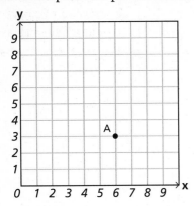

If she moves her pencil 3 units to the right and 2 units down, what will be the location of her pencil?

(A) (1, 9)   (C) (8, 0)

(B) (9, 1)   (D) (3, 1)

> Use your pencil to mark the movements on the grid from point *A* to the right and down.

31. Point *M* on the coordinate grid represents the location of Michelle's house. Point *N* represents the location of Nieka's house.

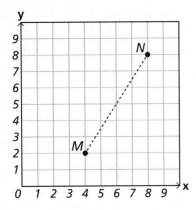

What is the location of a point that is halfway between Michelle's house and Nieka's house?

(A) (4, 5)

(B) (5, 6)

(C) (6, 5)

(D) (6, 8)

> Write down the ordered pairs for point *M* and point *N*. Then find the *x*-value that is halfway between the two first numbers in the ordered pairs and the *y*-value that is halfway between the two second numbers.

Standardized Test Tutor: Math (Grade 6) © 2009 by Michael Priestley, Scholastic Teaching Resources

Standardized Test Tutor: Math (Grade 6) © 2009 by Michael Priestley, Scholastic Teaching Resources

Test Tutor says:

32. A fire escape runs down the back of a building that is shaped like a rectangle.

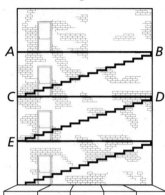

Find the line segments $\overline{BC}$ and $\overline{DE}$ in the diagram. Then think about how they are related.

If $\overline{AB}$ and $\overline{CD}$ are parallel to the roof of the building, what is the relationship between $\overline{BC}$ and $\overline{DE}$?

Ⓐ They are perpendicular.   Ⓒ They are intersecting.

Ⓑ They are parallel.   Ⓓ They are complementary.

33. What will be the position of point A if $\triangle ABC$ is reflected across the line $x = 4$?

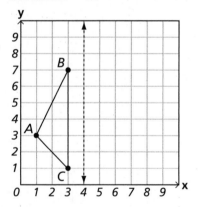

Remember that a reflection will create a mirror image on the other side of the dotted line. Each point on the reflection will be the same distance away from the line as the corresponding point of the original shape.

Ⓐ (5, 3)   Ⓒ (3, 5)

Ⓑ (6, 3)   Ⓓ (7, 3)

34. The perimeter of a cattle ranch is 14.6 kilometers. The rancher plans to fence the entire perimeter as well as a square corral with sides that are 65 meters long. How much fencing does the rancher need in all?

Ⓐ 14.86 km   Ⓒ 18.825 km

Ⓑ 17.2 km   Ⓓ 79.6 km

The total amount of fencing will enclose the ranch and the corral. The corral is a square with four sides of equal length. 1 kilometer = 1,000 meters.

35. A plane takes off from Detroit at 7:15 A.M. It lands in Miami, Florida, 4 hours 28 minutes later and spends 2 hours 7 minutes at the Miami airport before departing for New York City. The plane lands in New York City after a flight of 2 hours 55 minutes. At what time does the plane reach New York City?

Ⓐ 4:30 P.M.   Ⓒ 5:15 P.M.

Ⓑ 4:45 P.M.   Ⓓ 5:45 P.M.

> Write down each step in this problem. Add the hours and minutes to each new time to find the arrival time.

36. Which net could be folded to form a cube?

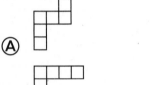

Ⓐ

Ⓒ

Ⓑ

Ⓓ

> Imagine folding up the net to see if it will make a cube.

37. Students at Allenwood Middle School come from four towns. The circle graph shows the percentage of students who come from each town.

Hometowns of Students at Allenwood Middle School

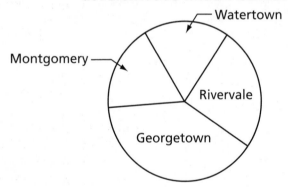

Which statement is supported by the graph?

Ⓐ There are more students from Georgetown than from Montgomery and Watertown combined.

Ⓑ There are more students from Rivervale than from Montgomery and Watertown combined.

Ⓒ There are more students from Georgetown than from all the other schools combined.

Ⓓ More than half of the students are from Georgetown.

> Look at the graph and estimate the fraction of the circle represented by each town. Then read each statement carefully.

Standardized Test Tutor: Math (Grade 6) © 2009 by Michael Priestley, Scholastic Teaching Resources

38. Sam's Lunch Wagon offers five kinds of sandwiches. The circle graph shows the percentage of sales for each kind of sandwich for the month of January.

Sandwiches Sold in January

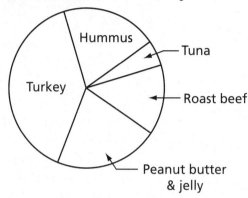

Which statement is supported by the graph?

Ⓐ More than half of the sandwiches sold were turkey sandwiches.

Ⓑ Sam's sold more peanut better and jelly sandwiches than hummus and roast beef combined.

Ⓒ Peanut butter and jelly and hummus sandwiches combined made up about half of the sandwiches sold.

Ⓓ Sam's sold more turkey sandwiches than all the other kinds of sandwiches combined.

> Look at the graph and estimate the fraction of the circle represented by each kind of sandwich. Then read each statement carefully. Cross out the statements that you know are wrong.

39. Mr. Kinley's students took a test. Their scores are shown in the stem-and-leaf plot below.

Math Test Scores

Stem	Leaf
9	0 0 1 2 4 7 7 8
8	0 2 2 3 5 6 6
7	3 6 6 8 9
6	8
5	4 9

> To read a stem-and-leaf plot, join each "stem" on the left with each "leaf" on the right. For example, the first score in the top row is 90. The two scores in the bottom row are 54 and 59.

How many students earned a score of 80 or higher on the test?

Ⓐ 5   Ⓒ 8

Ⓑ 7   Ⓓ 15

40. Crystal takes a tile from a bag that contains 26 tiles, one with each letter of the alphabet. She removes the tile from the bag and then takes one more tile. How many different permutations of letters is it possible for her to get with these two tiles?

- Ⓐ 51
- Ⓑ 325
- Ⓒ 650
- Ⓓ 676

After Crystal draws one tile from the bag, there are 25 tiles left. Each of the 26 letters available for the first draw may be combined with any one of the remaining 25 letters.

41. Tyrone rolls two number cubes numbered 1 to 6. What is the probability that both number cubes will land on the same number?

- Ⓐ $\frac{1}{2}$
- Ⓑ $\frac{1}{6}$
- Ⓒ $\frac{1}{12}$
- Ⓓ $\frac{1}{36}$

Each number cube may land on any of its six sides: 1, 2, 3, 4, 5, or 6. The probability of two events happening (rolling the same number on each cube) is the probability of one event times the probability of the other.

42. Rachel flipped a coin 10 times. It landed on heads 7 of the 10 times. If she tosses the coin again, which statement can be made about the probable outcome?

- Ⓐ The experimental probability of the coin landing on heads is 50 percent.
- Ⓑ The experimental and theoretical probability that the coin will land on heads is the same.
- Ⓒ The theoretical probability of the coin landing on heads is 10 percent.
- Ⓓ The experimental probability that the coin will land on heads is 70 percent.

Remember that *experimental* probability is based on the results of an experiment or trial.

Standardized Test Tutor: Math (Grade 6) © 2009 by Michael Priestley, Scholastic Teaching Resources

Test Tutor says:

43. Zach measured the height of all the trees in his yard. The stem-and-leaf plot shows the heights of the trees (in feet).

Tree Height (ft)

Stem	Leaf
5	2 2
4	4 5 8
3	4
2	2 7
1	8

What is the mean height of the trees?

Ⓐ 38 ft

Ⓑ 44 ft

Ⓒ 52 ft

Ⓓ 342 ft

> To find the mean, add the heights of all the trees listed in the stem-and-leaf plot and divide by the number of trees.

44. Raphael took a survey of his classmates to find out how many cousins they had. The results are shown in the graph below.

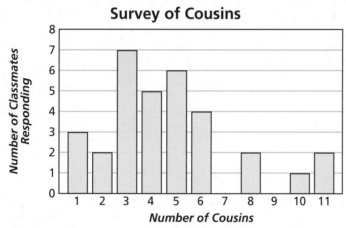

Survey of Cousins

What is the mode of these data?

Ⓐ 3

Ⓑ 4

Ⓒ 6

Ⓓ 7

> To find the mode, look for the data value that appears most often in a set of data.

45. Ron takes a poll to see which candidates his classmates plan to vote for to be class president. The results are displayed in the graph below.

Ron's Poll of Voters

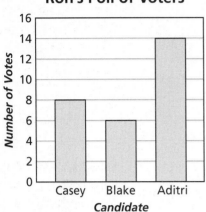

How many more students plan to vote for Aditri than for Casey?

Ⓐ 3

Ⓑ 6

Ⓒ 8

Ⓓ 14

> To read the bar graph, find the bar for each candidate (named at the bottom) and read across from the top of the bar to the number of votes on the left side (or vertical axis).

46. Fred is helping his little brother stack wooden blocks to make a staircase. They start by using a total of 6 blocks as shown below.

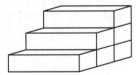

If they continue to build the staircase until the top stair is 10 blocks tall, how many blocks will they use in all?

Ⓐ 16

Ⓑ 45

Ⓒ 55

Ⓓ 60

> Note that each stair uses one block more than the previous stair, and there are 10 steps total.

Standardized Test Tutor: Math (Grade 6) © 2009 by Michael Priestley, Scholastic Teaching Resources

Test Tutor says:

47. Audrey has 200 feet of rope. She wants to cut the rope into a number of 6-foot pieces (*m*) and 2-foot pieces (*n*). Which equation could she use to find how many pieces she can cut from the rope?

Ⓐ $6m + 2n = 200$

Ⓑ $6m - 2n = 200$

Ⓒ $2n(6m) = 200$

Ⓓ $200 \div 6m = 2n$

> Think of the problem this way: Audrey wants to cut two different lengths of ropes: *m* number of lengths × 6 feet and *n* number of lengths × 2 feet.

48. Which expression is equivalent to $4 + 3(a + b)$?

Ⓐ $4 + 3a + 3b$

Ⓑ $4 + 3ab$

Ⓒ $4 + 3a + b$

Ⓓ $7a + 7b$

> Remember that the values in parentheses must both be multiplied by the number outside the parentheses.

49. A computer program is set up so that if you input a number, it will generate a number that is twice as large. Which graph shows the relationship between *x*, the number input into the program, and *y*, the number that the computer generates?

> Write an equation describing the rule: any number that goes into the program (*x*) comes out as a number that is twice as large (*y*). Then solve the equation to find ordered pairs. Use the ordered pairs to identify the graph of the line.

Ⓐ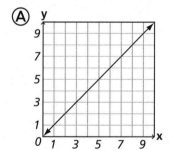

Ⓒ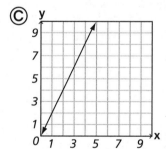

Ⓑ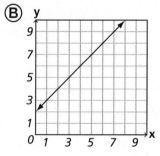

Ⓓ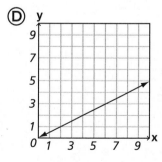

50. Solve for *x*:

$$\frac{36}{x} = 4$$

Ⓐ *x* = 9   Ⓒ *x* = 40

Ⓑ *x* = 32   Ⓓ *x* = 144

To solve the equation, you must first get *x* on one side of the equation by itself. Rewrite as $\frac{4}{1}$ and cross-multiply to solve the proportion.

51. The maximum number of students that can fit on a bus is 40. Mrs. Robertson's class of 27 students will ride on the bus. Mrs. Robertson writes the following inequality to find how many more students can fit on the bus.

$$s + 27 \leq 40$$

What is the solution to the inequality?

Ⓐ *s* ≥ 67   Ⓒ *s* ≥ 13

Ⓑ *s* ≤ 67   Ⓓ *s* ≤ 13

To solve the inequality, you must first get *s* on one side of the inequality by itself. What must you add or subtract to both sides to isolate the variable?

52. A spout pours water into a tank at a rate of 1 pound per minute. The empty tank weighs 3 pounds. The relationship between time (*x*) and the weight of the tank (*y*) can be expressed as the equation *y* = *x* + 3 when *x* ≥ 0. Which graph shows this relationship?

Focus on the equation *y* = *x* + 3. Solve this equation to find ordered pairs, and use the pairs to identify the graph of the line.

Ⓐ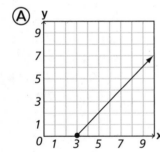

Ⓒ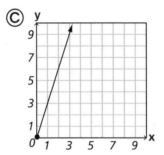

Ⓑ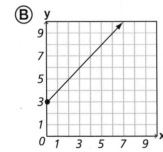

Ⓓ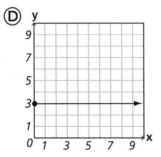

Standardized Test Tutor: Math (Grade 6) © 2009 by Michael Priestley, Scholastic Teaching Resources

53. Jorge and Warren have both been playing basketball for five years. The chart below shows the average percentage of free throw shots they have made each year.

Free Throw Percentage		
Year	Jorge	Warren
1	20%	26%
2	24%	28%
3	30%	31%
4	35%	33%
5	40%	36%

Which statement is supported by the information in the table?

Ⓐ   Warren has been consistently better at making free throws than Jorge.

Ⓑ   Jorge has been consistently better at making free throws than Warren.

Ⓒ   Jorge's free throw average has improved more quickly than Warren's.

Ⓓ   Warren's and Jorge's free throw averages have both improved at about the same rate.

> Look at the table carefully. What trends or changes do you see in Jorge's performance and Warren's performance from one year to the next one?

54. A circular crater has a diameter of 8,145 feet. Which is a reasonable estimate of its circumference?

Ⓐ   2,560 ft

Ⓑ   25,600 ft

Ⓒ   256,000 ft

Ⓓ   2,560,000 ft

> The word *estimate* tells you to think of this problem in rounded numbers. The circumference of a circle is $\pi \times$ the diameter. π is a little more than 3.

End of Test 1   STOP

Standardized Test Tutor: Math (Grade 6) © 2009 by Michael Priestley, Scholastic Teaching Resources

Directions: Read each question. Look at the Test Tutor's tip for answering the question. Then find the answer. You may do your work on this page or on scrap paper. Mark your answer by filling in the bubble.

1. Which statement about the decimal 0.6 is true?

   Ⓐ $0.6 < \frac{6}{12}$

   Ⓑ $0.6 > \frac{8}{20}$

   Ⓒ $0.6 > 0.63$

   Ⓓ $0.6 = \frac{10}{6}$

> To compare fractions and decimals, change them to all fractions with the same denominators or to all decimals.

2. Juno's bill for dinner is $22, and she wants to leave a 15% tip. If she hands the waiter $40 and gets her change back, how much of the change should she keep?

   Ⓐ $3.30

   Ⓑ $14.70

   Ⓒ $16.50

   Ⓓ $25.30

> Read the problem carefully to make sure you know what the question is asking for.

3. Which statement about the integer −5 is true?

   Ⓐ $-5 < -4$ Ⓒ $-5 = 5$

   Ⓑ $-5 < -6$ Ⓓ $-5 > 3$

> Compare negative and positive integers by putting them on a number line.

4. The population of Venezuela is about 25,731,000. Which digit in this number is in the millions place?

   Ⓐ 2

   Ⓑ 3

   Ⓒ 5

   Ⓓ 7

> Write the number in expanded form to find place values.

5. At the Stenson School, there are 109 students in the sixth grade, 113 students in the seventh grade, 137 in the eighth grade, and 123 students in the ninth grade. In which grade can the students be evenly divided into more than one group?

Ⓐ sixth grade

Ⓑ seventh grade

Ⓒ eighth grade

Ⓓ ninth grade

> Look for the composite (or non-prime) number.

6. What is the least common multiple of 12 and 32?

Ⓐ 12

Ⓑ 64

Ⓒ 96

Ⓓ 384

> List the multiples of both numbers and compare the lists.

7. What is the prime factorization of 625?

Ⓐ 6.25×10^2

Ⓑ 5^4

Ⓒ 25×25

Ⓓ $5 \times 5 \times 5 \times 5 \times 5$

> Remember that a prime number has only two factors, 1 and itself.

8. Simpson's Pet Shop sells groups of angelfish and goldfish together, as shown below.

Simpson's Pet Shop Aquarium Fish			
	Group 1	Group 2	Group 3
Angelfish	3	5	8
Goldfish	12	20	32

What is the ratio of angelfish to goldfish in each group?

Ⓐ 1 to 9

Ⓑ 1 to 4

Ⓒ 3 to 5

Ⓓ 3 to 32

> Compare the numbers in each column to find the ratio, then simplify.

Standardized Test Tutor: Math (Grade 6) © 2009 by Michael Priestley, Scholastic Teaching Resources

Test Tutor says:

9. A cafe bakes 3 dozen cookies each day. During a normal year (365 days), how many cookies does the cafe bake?

   Ⓐ 1,095

   Ⓑ 3,285

   Ⓒ 4,380

   Ⓓ 13,140

Write a number sentence or equation to help you solve the problem.

10. A chemist needs to divide $\frac{8}{5}$ liters of acid into test tubes that can each hold $\frac{1}{8}$ liter of acid. How many test tubes can the chemist fill?

   Ⓐ $\frac{1}{5}$ Ⓒ 5

   Ⓑ $1\frac{19}{40}$ Ⓓ $12\frac{4}{5}$

Look for key words to help you solve the problem.

11. A baker has a sack of flour that weighs 6.28 kilograms. If a batch of biscuits requires 0.4 kilograms of flour, how many batches of biscuits can the baker make with the sack of flour?

   Ⓐ 1.57   Ⓒ 15.7

   Ⓑ 2.512   Ⓓ 157

When working with decimals, make sure to place the decimal point correctly.

12. Emiko walks 3 miles in 45 minutes. At this rate, how many minutes will it take her to walk 5 miles?

   Ⓐ 27 minutes   Ⓒ 63 minutes

   Ⓑ 60 minutes   Ⓓ 75 minutes

Find the number of minutes per mile and apply that to 5 miles.

13. As an airplane flies higher, the outside temperature drops. Five minutes after a plane takes off, the outside temperature is $-7°$C. Two minutes later, the temperature is $-12°$C. What was the change in temperature during those two minutes?

   Ⓐ $-19°$C

   Ⓑ $-5°$C

   Ⓒ $5°$C

   Ⓓ $19°$C

To determine the amount of change, find the difference between the two numbers.

Standardized Test Tutor: Math (Grade 6) © 2009 by Michael Priestley, Scholastic Teaching Resources

Standardized Test Tutor: Math (Grade 6) © 2009 by Michael Priestley, Scholastic Teaching Resources

14. The Robbins family is driving a total of 1,504 miles to visit Aunt Mindy. On the first day of their trip, they drive 479 miles. On the second day, they drive 542 miles. Which is the best estimate of how many miles they will need to drive on the third day to reach Aunt Mindy's?

Ⓐ   300

Ⓑ   400

Ⓒ   500

Ⓓ   600

> In a question that asks for the *best estimate*, you can round the numbers to solve the problem.

15. Evaluate $2 + (3 + 3)^2 \div 4 - 1$ using order of operations.

Ⓐ $8\frac{1}{2}$

Ⓑ   10

Ⓒ $12\frac{2}{3}$

Ⓓ   15

> Remember the order of operations (PEMDAS).

16. Jake has 6 nickels. To find the total amount of money (M) he has, he writes the equation $5 + 5 + 5 + 5 + 5 + 5 = M$. What is another way to express this equation?

Ⓐ $5^6 = M$ Ⓒ $6^5 = M$

Ⓑ $5^2 = M$ Ⓓ $5(6) = M$

> Find the value of the equation and look for another way to express it.

17. Jill, Charese, Misha, and Nate are playing a card game with a deck of 52 cards. Jill deals out all the cards so that each player has the same number. Misha plays first. On his turn, he gives 2 cards to Jill. Next, Jill gives 3 cards to Charese. How many cards does Jill have after her turn?

Ⓐ   8

Ⓑ   10

Ⓒ   12

Ⓓ   14

> Write a number sentence to include each step in this problem.

18. A building that is 64 meters tall has 20 stories of equal height. Between each ceiling and the floor of the story above is a space of 0.7 meter for pipes and ventilation, and each floor itself is 0.14 meter thick, as shown in the diagram.

0.14 m { floor
0.7 m { space for pipes and ventilation

ceiling

h {

floor

What is the height (h) from floor to ceiling of each story in the building?

Ⓐ   2.36 m

Ⓑ   2.64 m

Ⓒ   2.99 m

Ⓓ   4.04 m

Find the height of each story and then subtract the spaces between floors that you see in the diagram.

19. A bucket holds 6 gallons of water. About how many liters of water does it hold? (1 gallon = 3.79 liters)

Ⓐ   1.5 L   Ⓒ   18 L

Ⓑ   6 L   Ⓓ   24 L

Notice the word *about*. That means you can round the numbers to solve the problem.

20. A rectangular mirror is 6 feet high and 2 feet wide. What is the perimeter of the mirror?

Ⓐ   6 ft   Ⓒ   12 ft

Ⓑ   8 ft   Ⓓ   16 ft

Don't confuse perimeter and area. The perimeter is the distance around the outside of a figure.

21. A rectangular field has an area of 494 m². If its width is 19 meters, which is the best estimate of the field's length?

Ⓐ   20 m

Ⓑ   25 m

Ⓒ   230 m

Ⓓ   10,000 m

Using the formula for area, work backward to find the length of the field.

Standardized Test Tutor: Math (Grade 6) © 2009 by Michael Priestley, Scholastic Teaching Resources

Test Tutor says:

22. What is the volume of this rectangular box?

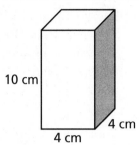

10 cm

4 cm

4 cm

Ⓐ 18 cm³

Ⓑ 40 cm³

Ⓒ 160 cm³

Ⓓ 192 cm³

> The formula for volume is length × width × height.

23. A day-care center is putting a fence around a circular play area. If the diameter of the play area is 20 meters, what is the length of fencing needed?

Ⓐ 10π m

Ⓑ 20π m

Ⓒ 100π m

Ⓓ 400π m

> The amount of fencing will be the circumference of the play area.

24. What is the measure of ∠NOP?

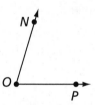

N

O

P

Ⓐ 73°

Ⓑ 87°

Ⓒ 107°

Ⓓ 163°

> Use a protractor to measure the angle.

25. Which triangle is an obtuse triangle?

Ⓐ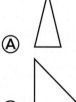

Ⓑ

Ⓒ

Ⓓ

> Don't confuse obtuse angles with acute or right angles.

26. Which of these could describe a trapezoid?

Ⓐ a three-sided figure with two equal sides

Ⓑ a four-sided figure with one set of parallel sides

Ⓒ a five-sided figure with one set of parallel sides

Ⓓ a quadrilateral with two sets of parallel sides

Draw a picture of each shape as described if it will help you answer the question.

27. A square courtyard is bordered by paths and has two diagonal paths running across it, as shown below.

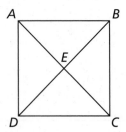

Which section of path is congruent to $\overline{EC}$?

Ⓐ $\overline{AE}$

Ⓑ $\overline{AD}$

Ⓒ $\overline{BD}$

Ⓓ $\overline{CD}$

Think about the properties of a square as you look at the line segments in the figure.

28. Malea has two wooden blocks. One is a triangular pyramid, and one is a rectangular prism. How many more faces does a rectangular prism have than the triangular pyramid?

Ⓐ 1

Ⓑ 2

Ⓒ 3

Ⓓ 4

Make a quick sketch of each figure to compare the number of faces.

Standardized Test Tutor: Math (Grade 6) © 2009 by Michael Priestley, Scholastic Teaching Resources

29. The shaded region of the coordinate grid represents a garden.

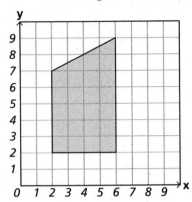

Find the ordered pair for each vertex, or corner, of the figure and compare them to the answer choices.

Which ordered pairs represent the vertices of the garden?

Ⓐ (2, 2), (2, 7), (2, 6), (9, 6)

Ⓑ (2, 2), (7, 2), (6, 2), (9, 6)

Ⓒ (2, 2), (7, 2), (2, 6), (9, 6)

Ⓓ (2, 2), (2, 7), (6, 2), (6, 9)

30. A hotel is installing a rectangular pool in the courtyard, as shown on the grid below. A fountain will be placed in the center of the pool.

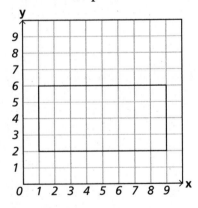

What will be the coordinates of the center point of the fountain?

Ⓐ (5, 4)

Ⓑ (9, 4)

Ⓒ (4, 5)

Ⓓ (5, 2)

Draw diagonals to find the center of the rectangle.

Test Tutor says:

31. The map below shows the center of Amesville.

Which two streets are perpendicular to each other?

Ⓐ   Main St. and Broad St.

Ⓑ   Center St. and Broad St.

Ⓒ   Center St. and Oak St.

Ⓓ   Oak St. and Main St.

Look carefully at the map to find the answer.

32. If quadrilateral *ABCD* is translated 2 units to the right, what will be the coordinates of point *B*?

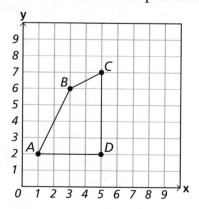

Ⓐ   (5, 6)

Ⓑ   (7, 7)

Ⓒ   (1, 6)

Ⓓ   (7, 6)

Draw the translated figure on the grid to help find the answer.

Standardized Test Tutor: Math (Grade 6) © 2009 by Michael Priestley, Scholastic Teaching Resources

Test
Tutor
says:

33. A puppy weighs 5.5 ounces at birth. A year later, it weighs
6 pounds 4 ounces. How much did the puppy's weight increase
during that year?

Ⓐ 0.9 lb

Ⓑ 5 lb 8.5 oz

Ⓒ 5 lb 14.5 oz

Ⓓ 6 lb 9.5 oz

Remember there are
16 ounces in a pound.

34. From 10:00 A.M. to 4:00 P.M. on Tuesday, the outside
temperature increased by 27°F. On average, how many
degrees did the temperature increase each hour?

Ⓐ 3.5°F

Ⓑ 4.5°F

Ⓒ 5.4°F

Ⓓ 6.75°F

Choose the correct
operation to find the
number of degrees per hour.

35. The drawing below is a perspective drawing of a wall vanishing
into the distance.

What would this wall look like from above?

Ⓐ

Ⓑ

Ⓒ

Ⓓ

Use a piece of paper or any
rectangular object to help
visualize the figure.

Standardized Test Tutor: Math (Grade 6) © 2009 by Michael Priestley, Scholastic Teaching Resources

Test
Tutor
says:

The graph below shows the monthly sales of spaghetti at Alfredo's Pasta Shop. Use the graph to answer questions 36–37.

Alfredo's Spaghetti Sales

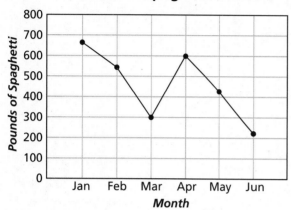

36. In which month did Alfredo's sell the most spaghetti?

Ⓐ January   Ⓒ March

Ⓑ February   Ⓓ April

Look carefully at the line graph to find the answer.

37. In which period did Alfredo's spaghetti sales decrease the most?

Ⓐ January to February

Ⓑ February to March

Ⓒ April to May

Ⓓ May to June

Think about the key words in this problem: *decrease the most.*

38. The heights of all the players on the Tigers Soccer Team are shown in the line plot below.

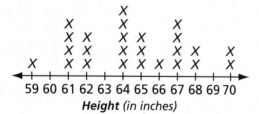

How many players are at least 65 inches tall?

Ⓐ 3   Ⓒ 12

Ⓑ 9   Ⓓ 16

Note that this question asks how many players are *at least* 65 inches tall, which includes 65 inches.

Standardized Test Tutor: Math (Grade 6) © 2009 by Michael Priestley, Scholastic Teaching Resources

39. Gillian has three sweatshirts (blue, pink, and white) and three pairs of shorts (black, yellow, and green). Which tree diagram best shows all of the possible combinations of one sweatshirt and one pair of shorts that Gillian can wear?

> Remember that a tree diagram has a separate path showing each possible combination.

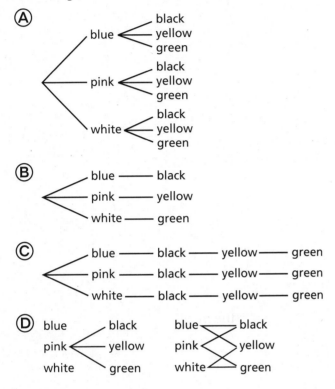

Ⓐ
blue — black, yellow, green
pink — black, yellow, green
white — black, yellow, green

Ⓑ
blue — black
pink — yellow
white — green

Ⓒ
blue — black — yellow — green
pink — black — yellow — green
white — black — yellow — green

Ⓓ
blue — black
pink — yellow
white — green

blue — black
pink — yellow
white — green

40. Marshall wants to order an ice cream sundae from Sunny's Ice Cream Shop. The sundae will have one flavor of ice cream, one topping, and one sauce. How many possible combinations of one ice cream, one topping, and one sauce can he choose from?

> Draw a diagram if that will help you solve this problem.

Sunny's Ice Cream Sundae Choices		
Ice cream	Toppings	Sauce
Chocolate	Peanuts	Hot fudge
Vanilla	Sprinkles	Caramel
Strawberry	Bananas	
Mint	Raspberries	

Ⓐ 10

Ⓑ 16

Ⓒ 24

Ⓓ 32

41. A gumball machine contains 8 red gumballs, 4 yellow gumballs, 3 green gumballs, and 9 blue gumballs. If a customer chooses one gumball randomly, what is the probability that the gumball will be red?

(A) $\frac{1}{2}$ (C) $\frac{1}{6}$

(B) $\frac{1}{3}$ (D) $\frac{1}{8}$

Simplify your answer to the lowest terms.

42. A bag contains 3 blue marbles and 7 yellow marbles. A box contains 5 blue marbles and 3 yellow marbles. Alan picks one marble at random from the bag and one marble at random from the box. What is the theoretical probability that both of the marbles he picks will be blue?

(A) $\frac{3}{16}$ (C) $\frac{15}{21}$

(B) $\frac{8}{10}$ (D) $\frac{37}{40}$

Remember that the probability of two independent events happening is the probability of one event times the probability of the other event.

43. Dr. Ragin checked the water temperature in 10 different lakes near his home. His results are shown in the table below.

Lake	Temperature (°F)
A	62
B	61
C	61
D	63
E	65
F	62
G	61
H	60
I	61
J	63

The range of a set of data is the difference between the highest and lowest data values.

What is the range of the temperatures Dr. Ragin found?

(A) 1°F   (C) 61°F

(B) 5°F   (D) 65°F

44. Amal compares the prices of shoes at a store, as shown below.

$130 $249 $95 $70

$149 $125 $249 $65

$310 $90 $79 $129

What is the median price of the shoes?

Ⓐ $245

Ⓑ $145

Ⓒ $127

Ⓓ $125

> Remember that the median is the value in the exact middle of a range of values when they are put in order from least to greatest.

45. At Northside Middle School, a total of 600 students voted for the new school color. The results are shown in the graph below.

School Color Voting Results

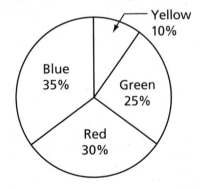

How many more students voted for blue than for yellow?

Ⓐ 25   Ⓒ 210

Ⓑ 150   Ⓓ 575

> To help solve this problem, find the number of students represented by each section of the circle graph.

46. Flora's parents plan to increase her allowance each year based on a pattern, as shown below.

Flora's Allowance

Year	1	2	3	4	5
Allowance ($)	5	9	13	17	21

Which expression shows how to find Flora's allowance in year n?

Ⓐ $n + 4$

Ⓑ $2n + 5$

Ⓒ $3n + 4$

Ⓓ $4n + 1$

> Using the numbers in the table, try the expression in each answer choice to find the one that works.

47. Simplify the expression:

$$10x + 4 - 4x^2 + 8 + 6x^2$$

Ⓐ $24x^2$

Ⓑ $20x^2 + 12$

Ⓒ $10x^2 + 10x + 12$

Ⓓ $2x^2 + 10x + 12$

> Combine like terms.

48. Monique has a piece of paper that is p centimeters tall and q centimeters wide. She tapes another 2 centimeters of paper to the top. The area of the paper can now be expressed as $q \times (p + 2)$. Which of these is equivalent to this expression?

Ⓐ $q \times (2 + p)$

Ⓑ $(q \times p) + 2$

Ⓒ $q + (p \times 2)$

Ⓓ $(q + p) \times 2$

> Focus on the expression $q \times (p + 2)$ to find an equivalent.

Standardized Test Tutor: Math (Grade 6) © 2009 by Michael Priestley, Scholastic Teaching Resources

49. What is the value of n in the input-output table?

Input	2	5	8	n
Output	10	25	40	35

Ⓐ 5

Ⓑ 7

Ⓒ 11

Ⓓ 13

> Use the numbers you know to find the rule for this table and determine the missing number.

50. Solve for w:

$$4w - 3 = 11$$

Ⓐ $w = 2$ Ⓒ $w = 32$

Ⓑ $w = 3.5$ Ⓓ $w = 56$

> To solve for w, isolate the variable on one side of the equation.

51. Emily wants to save at least $500 over the summer. She makes $140 babysitting and decides to make the rest of the money by selling flowers. For each bunch of flowers she sells, she makes $5. Emily writes the following inequality to find the minimum number of bunches of flowers (b) she will need to sell to make at least $500:

$$140 + 5b \geq 500$$

What is the solution to the inequality?

Ⓐ $b \leq 128$ Ⓒ $b \leq 72$

Ⓑ $b \geq 128$ Ⓓ $b \geq 72$

> To solve for b, isolate the variable on one side of the inequality.

52. The table below shows the distance traveled by a car over time.

Time in minutes (t)	2	5	6	7
Distance in miles (d)	1	2.5	3	3.5

Which equation shows the relationship between the time (t) and distance (d) traveled by the car?

Ⓐ $d = t - 1$ Ⓒ $d = \frac{1}{2}t$

Ⓑ $d = t + 3$ Ⓓ $d = 2t$

> Using the numbers in the table, try the equation in each answer choice to find the one that works.

53. A movie theater notes the ticket sales for a new movie each week after its release.

New Movie Ticket Sales

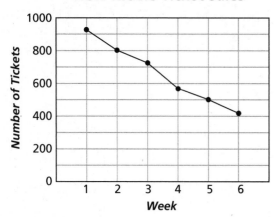

Based on the trend shown in the graph, what is the best prediction for ticket sales in week 8?

- (A) 200
- (B) 300
- (C) 400
- (D) 500

> Look at the line graph carefully to find the information you need.

54. A theater sells 12,050 tickets for a concert at $32 each. Which is the most reasonable estimate for the amount of money the theater made in ticket sales?

- (A) $3,856
- (B) $38,560
- (C) $385,600
- (D) $3,856,000

> Use rounding to find the best estimate for this problem.

End of Test 2 **STOP**

Standardized Test Tutor: Math (Grade 6) © 2009 by Michael Priestley, Scholastic Teaching Resources

Good Luck!

Directions: Choose the best answer to each question. Mark your answer by filling in the bubble.

1. Which number could be represented by point *F* on the number line?

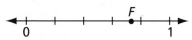

Ⓐ $\frac{17}{20}$

Ⓑ 0.36

Ⓒ $\frac{3}{4}$

Ⓓ $\frac{4}{10}$

2. Of the 25 students in Mr. McGarry's class, 36 percent are girls. Of the 20 students in Ms. Filipo's class, 55 percent are girls. How many more girls are in Ms. Filipo's class than Mr. McGarry's class?

Ⓐ 2

Ⓑ 5

Ⓒ 9

Ⓓ 11

3. During one week in the winter, Ms. Dolores recorded the following temperatures at noon of each day.

Monday	Tuesday	Wednesday	Thursday	Friday
−4°C	1°C	−2°C	−5°C	0°C

Which day had the highest temperature?

Ⓐ Tuesday

Ⓑ Wednesday

Ⓒ Thursday

Ⓓ Friday

4. A block of wood weighs 2,587.941 grams. Which digit in this number is in the hundredths place?

Ⓐ 1

Ⓑ 4

Ⓒ 5

Ⓓ 8

5. Marjel played in 7 basketball games last season and scored the same number of points in each game. Which of these could *not* have been her total number of points for the season?

Ⓐ 70

Ⓑ 63

Ⓒ 59

Ⓓ 56

6. A discount warehouse received a bulk shipment of 544 pairs of socks. The manager distributed them evenly into packages. Which of these could be the number of packages she made?

Ⓐ 68

Ⓑ 65

Ⓒ 60

Ⓓ 54

7. A population of mice triples every year. If there were 100 mice to begin with, how many mice would there be after 5 years?

Ⓐ 3^5

Ⓑ 100^5

Ⓒ 100×5^3

Ⓓ 100×3^5

Standardized Test Tutor: Math (Grade 6) © 2009 by Michael Priestley, Scholastic Teaching Resources

8. The chart below shows the number of balls and strikes a pitcher threw each inning in a baseball game.

Inning	Balls	Strikes
1	6	4
2	12	8
3	9	6
4	15	10

What was the ratio of balls to strikes in each inning?

Ⓐ 1 to 2

Ⓑ 4 to 3

Ⓒ 3 to 2

Ⓓ 3 to 5

9. A company produced 9,852 widgets one day and 8,494 widgets the next day. On the third day, one of the machines broke and only 95 widgets were produced. How many widgets did the company produce in the three days?

Ⓐ 18,346

Ⓑ 18,431

Ⓒ 18,441

Ⓓ 27,846

10. A farmer brings $20\frac{1}{2}$ pounds of almonds to a farmer's market. She sells $15\frac{2}{3}$ pounds. How many pounds of almonds does she have left?

Ⓐ $4\frac{2}{3}$

Ⓑ $4\frac{5}{6}$

Ⓒ $5\frac{2}{3}$

Ⓓ $5\frac{5}{6}$

11. Shakim has a tarp that covers 6.72 square meters and a tarp that covers 9.36 square meters. How many square meters can he cover with both tarps?

Ⓐ 15.08

Ⓑ 15.108

Ⓒ 16.08

Ⓓ 62.8992

12. If Victoria and Bloomsburg are 2.5 inches apart on the map, how many miles apart are they in reality?

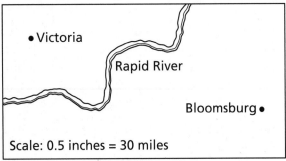

Victoria

Rapid River

Bloomsburg

Scale: 0.5 inches = 30 miles

Ⓐ 37.5

Ⓑ 60

Ⓒ 75

Ⓓ 150

13. In Fairbanks, Alaska, the temperature was $-10°C$ at noon. At midnight that night, it was $-25°C$. What was the change in temperature between noon and midnight?

Ⓐ $-35°C$

Ⓑ $-15°C$

Ⓒ $15°C$

Ⓓ $35°C$

Standardized Test Tutor: Math (Grade 6) © 2009 by Michael Priestley, Scholastic Teaching Resources

14. Mr. Escobar buys $1\frac{4}{9}$ pounds of white rice and $3\frac{4}{15}$ pounds of brown rice. Which is the best estimate of the weight of the white and brown rice together?

(A) 4 pounds

(B) $4\frac{1}{2}$ pounds

(C) $4\frac{3}{4}$ pounds

(D) 5 pounds

15. Evaluate $(6 + 4) \div 2 + 3 \times 6$ using order of operations.

(A) 12

(B) 23

(C) 26

(D) 48

16. Abdul has a number of CD's (C) with 15 songs on each CD. If $15 \times C = 840$, which equation could be used to find the number of CD's Abdul owns?

(A) $15 + C = 840$

(B) $15 \div C = 840$

(C) $840 + 15 = C$

(D) $840 \div 15 = C$

17. At Elmwood Middle School, $\frac{3}{4}$ of the students buy lunch at school. Of those students who buy lunch at school, $\frac{1}{3}$ buy a sandwich. If there are 180 students at Elmwood, how many buy a sandwich for lunch?

(A) 45

(B) 60

(C) 90

(D) 135

18. Roberto buys 2 boxes of cereal that cost $3.29 each. He also buys a quart of milk for $1.45. If Roberto uses a coupon for $0.50 off his purchase, how much does his purchase cost?

Ⓐ $4.24

Ⓑ $7.53

Ⓒ $8.03

Ⓓ $8.53

19. A recipe calls for 6 cups of milk. If Andre wants to double the recipe, how many **quarts** of milk will he need to buy?

Ⓐ 1.5 quarts

Ⓑ 3 quarts

Ⓒ 24 quarts

Ⓓ 48 quarts

20. A rectangular piece of paper is 8.5 inches wide and 11 inches long. What is the area of the piece of paper?

Ⓐ 19.5 in.^{2}

Ⓑ 39 in.^{2}

Ⓒ 46.75 in.^{2}

Ⓓ 93.5 in.^{2}

21. What is the area of the triangle?

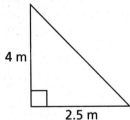

4 m

2.5 m

Ⓐ 5 m^2

Ⓑ 6.5 m^2

Ⓒ 10 m^2

Ⓓ 20 m^2

Standardized Test Tutor: Math (Grade 6) © 2009 by Michael Priestley, Scholastic Teaching Resources

22. One gallon of water weighs approximately 8.3 pounds. If a 5-gallon bucket weighs 0.6 pounds when empty, what is its weight when it is full of water?

Ⓐ 11.3 lb

Ⓑ 13.9 lb

Ⓒ 40.9 lb

Ⓓ 42.1 lb

23. Point *A* is in the center of the circle, and point *B* is on the edge of the circle. If the distance from point *A* to point *B* is 6 centimeters, what is the diameter of the circle?

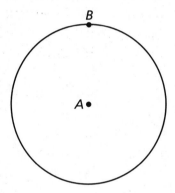

Ⓐ 3 cm

Ⓑ 6 cm

Ⓒ 12 cm

Ⓓ 6π cm

24. Estimate the measure of ∠*STU*.

Ⓐ 80°

Ⓑ 100°

Ⓒ 130°

Ⓓ 190°

25. A square is divided into two triangles, as shown below.

What type of triangle is the shaded triangle?

(A) right   (C) acute

(B) obtuse   (D) equilateral

26. Which term could *not* describe the polygon below?

(A) diamond   (C) parallelogram

(B) rectangle   (D) quadrilateral

27. $\overline{LN}$ divides quadrilateral *LMNO* into two congruent triangles. Which angle is congruent to $\angle OLN$?

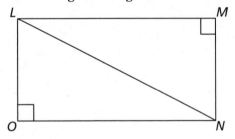

(A) $\angle OLM$

(B) $\angle NLM$

(C) $\angle MNL$

(D) $\angle LNO$

28. Which shape has only one flat surface?

Ⓐ cone

Ⓑ cylinder

Ⓒ triangular pyramid

Ⓓ rectangular prism

29. Marino plots three points on a coordinate grid, as shown below.

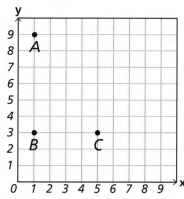

What are the coordinates of a fourth point that would create a rectangle with the three points on the grid?

Ⓐ (9, 5)

Ⓑ (9, 3)

Ⓒ (3, 9)

Ⓓ (5, 9)

30. Which triangle has vertices at points (2, 8), (5, 2), and (7, 4)?

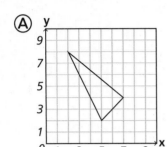

Ⓐ

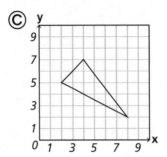

Ⓒ

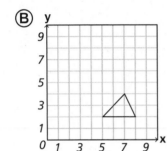

Ⓑ

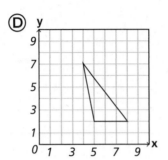

Ⓓ

31. A straw passes through the flat lid of a cup at a 75° angle.

What is the relationship between the line made by the straw and the plane made by the lid of the cup?

Ⓐ The line is parallel to the plane.

Ⓑ The line is perpendicular to the plane.

Ⓒ The line intersects the plane.

Ⓓ A line and a plane cannot have any of these relationships.

32. Which graph shows the result of rotating the triangle 180° about point *A*?

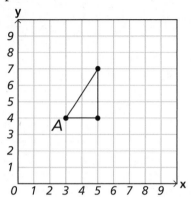

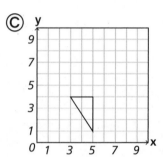

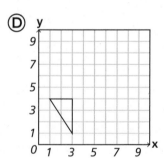

33. Sand weighs 90 lb/ft³. If a sandbox filled with sand is 15 feet long, 9 feet wide, and 2 feet deep, how much does the sand weigh?

   Ⓐ   116 lbs

   Ⓑ   270 lbs

   Ⓒ   2,340 lbs

   Ⓓ   24,300 lbs

34. A painter can paint 3 square meters of a wall in 15 minutes. If a wall is 4.5 meters wide and 2.5 meters tall, how long will the painter take to paint the entire wall?

Ⓐ 2.25 minutes

Ⓑ 35 minutes

Ⓒ 56.25 minutes

Ⓓ 168.75 minutes

35. Which net could be folded to form a square pyramid?

Ⓐ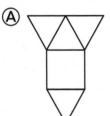

Ⓑ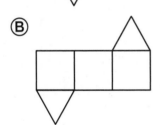

Ⓒ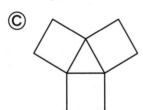

Ⓓ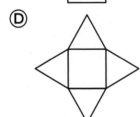

36. Darrell took a survey in his school about students' favorite kinds of movies. The graph below shows his results.

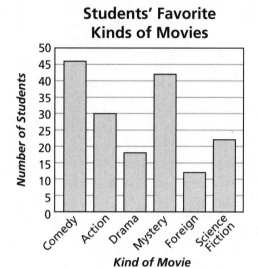

Which statement is supported by the graph?

Ⓐ More students chose comedy than chose action and drama combined.

Ⓑ More than twice as many students chose comedy as science fiction.

Ⓒ More students chose science fiction than chose foreign and drama combined.

Ⓓ More than twice as many students chose mystery as action.

37. Farrah counted the cars, trucks, and bicycles that passed her house for 30 minutes in the morning and 30 minutes in the afternoon. She recorded her results in the graph below.

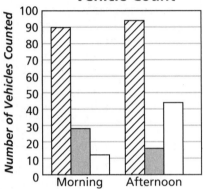

Which statement is supported by the graph?

(A)   Farrah counted more trucks in the afternoon than in the morning.

(B)   Farrah counted more bicycles in the afternoon than trucks and bicycles in the morning combined.

(C)   Farrah counted more cars in the afternoon than all of the other vehicles she counted combined.

(D)   Farrah counted more trucks in the morning than trucks and bicycles in the afternoon combined.

Standardized Test Tutor: Math (Grade 6) © 2009 by Michael Priestley, Scholastic Teaching Resources

38. A pet store buys 25 young rats and puts them on a special diet for a week. The weights of the rats before and after eating the special diet are shown in the stem-and-leaf plots below.

Weights of Rats Before Special Diet (grams)

Stem	Leaf
42	0 0 2 3 4 5 5 6
41	1 2 5 5 6
40	0 3 3 7 8 8 9
39	5 6 7 9 9

Weights of Rats After Special Diet (grams)

Stem	Leaf
44	0 1 2 2 3 4 9
43	1 3 5 5 7 8 8 9
42	0 0 3 7 8 8
41	5 6 7 9

After eating the special diet, how many rats weighed more than the heaviest rat weighed before the special diet?

Ⓐ 15
Ⓑ 18
Ⓒ 21
Ⓓ 25

39. Jamal performs an experiment. On each turn, he chooses a marble at random from a bag that contains four marbles—one red (R), one yellow (Y), one green (G), and one blue (B)—and flips a coin that can land either on heads (H) or tails (T). What is the sample space of this experiment?

Ⓐ {4, 2}
Ⓑ {RY, GB, HT}
Ⓒ {RY, RG, RB, YG, YB, GB, HT}
Ⓓ {RH, RT, YH, YT, GH, GT, BH, BT}

40. Carrie buys four books. In how many different orders can she arrange them in a line on her shelf?

Ⓐ 8
Ⓑ 16
Ⓒ 24
Ⓓ 256

41. In a board game, each player spins the arrow on the spinner shown below to determine how many spaces to move. The sections of the spinner are congruent.

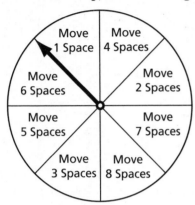

On a single spin, what is the probability that a player will move more than 5 spaces?

Ⓐ $\frac{3}{8}$

Ⓑ $\frac{1}{2}$

Ⓒ $\frac{5}{8}$

Ⓓ $\frac{3}{5}$

42. There are 9 girls and 6 boys in Ms. Hara's class. Ms. Hara puts all of her students' names in a hat. First she chooses one name at random and takes it out of the hat. Then she chooses another name at random from the hat. What is the theoretical probability that she will choose a girl's name first and a boy's name second?

Ⓐ 1

Ⓑ $\frac{6}{25}$

Ⓒ $\frac{9}{35}$

Ⓓ $\frac{36}{35}$

43. Mrs. Gillis's gym class takes a push-up test, and she writes down the number of push-ups each student is able to do. The list on her clipboard reads: 3, 8, 9, 10, 25, 2, 9, 5, 6, 23, 15, 12, 1, 3, 5, 14, 18, 21, 6, 3.

What is the median of these data?

Ⓐ 3

Ⓑ 8

Ⓒ 8.5

Ⓓ 9.15

44. The chart below shows the amount of rainfall the town of Edgarville received in each of the last six months.

Rainfall in Edgarville (cm)					
January	February	March	April	May	June
22	25	33	34	24	18

What is the mean amount of rain Edgarville received over the six months?

Ⓐ 16

Ⓑ 24

Ⓒ 24.5

Ⓓ 26

45. Jerome records the amount of money in his savings account at the end of each month. His records are shown below.

Jerome's Savings Account					
April	May	June	July	August	September
$240	$360	$520	$340	$280	$320

Jerome wants to show how the money in his account has changed over time. What is the best way for him to display his data?

Ⓐ circle graph

Ⓑ stem-and-leaf plot

Ⓒ line graph

Ⓓ line plot

46. Mrs. Lopez notices that there are lily pads beginning to grow on Long Pond behind her house. She decides to keep track of how many lily pads are on the pond each week. Her results are shown in the table below.

Lily Pads on Long Pond				
Week	1	2	3	4
Number of Lily Pads	32	62	92	122

If this pattern of growth continues, how many lily pads will be on the pond in week 7?

Ⓐ 152

Ⓑ 182

Ⓒ 202

Ⓓ 212

47. Manuel had $82 in his savings account. Then he deposited $25 in his account on May 1, and the account earned $0.02 interest each day after that. Which expression represents the amount of money in his account after n days?

Ⓐ $82 + $25 + $0.02

Ⓑ $82 + $25 + $0.02 + n

Ⓒ $82 + $25 + 0.02n$

Ⓓ ($82 + $25) $\times$ n + $0.02

48. Which expression is equivalent to $\dfrac{(5 + x) + x}{3(x + 4)}$?

Ⓐ $\dfrac{5 + 2x}{3x + 12}$

Ⓑ $\dfrac{5 + 2x}{3x + 4}$

Ⓒ $\dfrac{5x + x}{3x + 4}$

Ⓓ $\dfrac{5x + x^2}{3x + 12}$

Standardized Test Tutor: Math (Grade 6) © 2009 by Michael Priestley, Scholastic Teaching Resources

49. The rule for an input-output table states that an output will be 3 times the input, minus 1. Which input-output table follows this rule?

Ⓐ
Input	5	6	8
Output	16	19	25

Ⓑ
Input	4	7	9
Output	11	20	26

Ⓒ
Input	5	8	17
Output	2	3	6

Ⓓ
Input	4	16	22
Output	1	5	7

50. Solve for r:

$$6r = 18$$

Ⓐ $r = 3$

Ⓑ $r = 12$

Ⓒ $r = 24$

Ⓓ $r = 108$

51. An old bridge has a weight limit of 5,000 pounds. A truck carrying no cargo weighs 2,500 pounds including the driver. The truck will be loaded with 20-pound boxes. The inequality below shows the maximum number of boxes he can carry in the truck and still cross the bridge:

$$2,500 + 20b < 5,000$$

What is the solution to the inequality?

Ⓐ $b < 125$

Ⓑ $b > 125$

Ⓒ $b < 375$

Ⓓ $b > 375$

52. Wendy made the graph below to represent an equation.

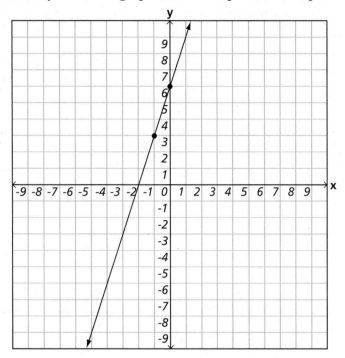

Which equation is represented by the graph?

Ⓐ $y = -3x - 2$

Ⓑ $y = -3x + 6$

Ⓒ $y = 3x - 2$

Ⓓ $y = 3x + 6$

Standardized Test Tutor: Math (Grade 6) © 2009 by Michael Priestley, Scholastic Teaching Resources

53. Jerry's Jams and Jellies is studying the effects of advertising on the sales of its new products. The table below shows the results of the study.

Product	Average sales before advertising (number of jars sold/day)	Average sales after advertising in the store (number of jars sold/day)	Average sales after advertising in the newspaper (number of jars sold/day)
Raspberry maple jelly	16	33	41
Orange honey marmalade	28	54	69
Ginger peach jam	20	39	51

Jerry's Jams and Jellies New Product Sales

Jerry's introduces a blueberry orange jam that sells an average of 12 jars per day before advertising. Based on the information in the table, what is the best prediction of how many jars per day Jerry's should expect to sell of the blueberry orange jam after advertising in the newspaper?

Ⓐ 24   Ⓒ 36

Ⓑ 30   Ⓓ 48

54. The Spanish club holds a bake sale to raise money for a field trip. The students in the club want to raise at least $325 over two days by selling brownies for $1.59 each. On the first day, they raise $155.82 by selling 98 brownies. Which is the most reasonable estimate of the number of brownies they must sell on the second day to raise a total of about $325?

Ⓐ 105   Ⓒ 85

Ⓑ 95   Ⓓ 75

End of Test 3 **STOP**

Standardized Test Tutor: Math (Grade 6) © 2009 by Michael Priestley, Scholastic Teaching Resources

Standardized Test Tutor: Math Grade 6

Answer Sheet

Student Name _____

Teacher Name _____

Test 1 2 3
(circle one)

1. Ⓐ Ⓑ Ⓒ Ⓓ   19. Ⓐ Ⓑ Ⓒ Ⓓ   37. Ⓐ Ⓑ Ⓒ Ⓓ

2. Ⓐ Ⓑ Ⓒ Ⓓ   20. Ⓐ Ⓑ Ⓒ Ⓓ   38. Ⓐ Ⓑ Ⓒ Ⓓ

3. Ⓐ Ⓑ Ⓒ Ⓓ   21. Ⓐ Ⓑ Ⓒ Ⓓ   39. Ⓐ Ⓑ Ⓒ Ⓓ

4. Ⓐ Ⓑ Ⓒ Ⓓ   22. Ⓐ Ⓑ Ⓒ Ⓓ   40. Ⓐ Ⓑ Ⓒ Ⓓ

5. Ⓐ Ⓑ Ⓒ Ⓓ   23. Ⓐ Ⓑ Ⓒ Ⓓ   41. Ⓐ Ⓑ Ⓒ Ⓓ

6. Ⓐ Ⓑ Ⓒ Ⓓ   24. Ⓐ Ⓑ Ⓒ Ⓓ   42. Ⓐ Ⓑ Ⓒ Ⓓ

7. Ⓐ Ⓑ Ⓒ Ⓓ   25. Ⓐ Ⓑ Ⓒ Ⓓ   43. Ⓐ Ⓑ Ⓒ Ⓓ

8. Ⓐ Ⓑ Ⓒ Ⓓ   26. Ⓐ Ⓑ Ⓒ Ⓓ   44. Ⓐ Ⓑ Ⓒ Ⓓ

9. Ⓐ Ⓑ Ⓒ Ⓓ   27. Ⓐ Ⓑ Ⓒ Ⓓ   45. Ⓐ Ⓑ Ⓒ Ⓓ

10. Ⓐ Ⓑ Ⓒ Ⓓ   28. Ⓐ Ⓑ Ⓒ Ⓓ   46. Ⓐ Ⓑ Ⓒ Ⓓ

11. Ⓐ Ⓑ Ⓒ Ⓓ   29. Ⓐ Ⓑ Ⓒ Ⓓ   47. Ⓐ Ⓑ Ⓒ Ⓓ

12. Ⓐ Ⓑ Ⓒ Ⓓ   30. Ⓐ Ⓑ Ⓒ Ⓓ   48. Ⓐ Ⓑ Ⓒ Ⓓ

13. Ⓐ Ⓑ Ⓒ Ⓓ   31. Ⓐ Ⓑ Ⓒ Ⓓ   49. Ⓐ Ⓑ Ⓒ Ⓓ

14. Ⓐ Ⓑ Ⓒ Ⓓ   32. Ⓐ Ⓑ Ⓒ Ⓓ   50. Ⓐ Ⓑ Ⓒ Ⓓ

15. Ⓐ Ⓑ Ⓒ Ⓓ   33. Ⓐ Ⓑ Ⓒ Ⓓ   51. Ⓐ Ⓑ Ⓒ Ⓓ

16. Ⓐ Ⓑ Ⓒ Ⓓ   34. Ⓐ Ⓑ Ⓒ Ⓓ   52. Ⓐ Ⓑ Ⓒ Ⓓ

17. Ⓐ Ⓑ Ⓒ Ⓓ   35. Ⓐ Ⓑ Ⓒ Ⓓ   53. Ⓐ Ⓑ Ⓒ Ⓓ

18. Ⓐ Ⓑ Ⓒ Ⓓ   36. Ⓐ Ⓑ Ⓒ Ⓓ   54. Ⓐ Ⓑ Ⓒ Ⓓ

Test **1** Answer Key

1. D	**12.** C	**23.** C	**34.** A	**45.** B
2. C	**13.** D	**24.** A	**35.** B	**46.** C
3. A	**14.** C	**25.** D	**36.** C	**47.** A
4. A	**15.** C	**26.** B	**37.** A	**48.** A
5. D	**16.** A	**27.** A	**38.** C	**49.** C
6. B	**17.** B	**28.** D	**39.** D	**50.** A
7. C	**18.** C	**29.** D	**40.** C	**51.** D
8. A	**19.** B	**30.** B	**41.** B	**52.** B
9. A	**20.** B	**31.** C	**42.** D	**53.** C
10. B	**21.** C	**32.** B	**43.** A	**54.** B
11. A	**22.** D	**33.** D	**44.** A	

Answer Key Explanations

1. Correct response: **D**
(*Compare and order whole numbers, fractions, and decimals*)

If the numbers are converted to fractions with a common denominator, then you can order them by the numerators from least to greatest: $\frac{5}{20}$, $0.3 = \frac{6}{20}$, $1 = \frac{20}{20}$, and $\frac{7}{5} = \frac{28}{20}$.

Incorrect choices:

A represents a misconception that all fractions are less than whole numbers, and it includes a computational error when comparing 0.3 and $\frac{5}{20}$.

B represents a misconception that all fractions are less than whole numbers.

C represents a computational error when comparing 0.3 and $\frac{5}{20}$.

2. Correct response: **C**
(*Compare, order, and use percents*)

To compare the sale prices, first apply the discount to the original price of each item. On sale, shoes cost the least: 40% of $60 = $24, so $60 − $24 = $36. All of the other items cost $40 or more.

Incorrect choices:

A The jeans cost $40.50 ($45 − $4.50).

B The sweater costs $40 ($50 − $10).

D The jacket costs $40 ($80 − $40).

3. Correct response: **A**
(*Compare, order, and use integers*)

These integers are in the correct order, with the least negative number first (−6) and the greatest positive number last (2).

3. (continued)
   Incorrect choices:

   B shows the numbers in order from greatest to least.

   C and **D** would be in order from least to greatest if the negative signs were ignored (or absolute value were being considered).

4. Correct Response: **A**
   (*Identify and use place value*)
   This number represents five hundred thirty-four thousand seven hundred twenty-six, or $500,000 + 30,000 + 4,000 + 700 + 20 + 6$. The **3** represents the ten thousands place.

   Incorrect choices:

   B The 4 is in the thousands place.

   C The 5 is in the hundred thousands place.

   D The 7 represents hundreds.

5. Correct response: **D**
   (*Identify and describe prime and composite numbers, and prime factors*)
   Factors of 56 are 7 and 8, but 8 is not a prime number; 8 can be reduced to $2 \times 2 \times 2$, or 2^3.

   Incorrect responses:

   A 8×7 is not reduced to prime factors.

   B $2 \times 4 \times 7$ is not reduced to prime factors.

   C The factors have been reduced improperly.

6. Correct response: **B**
   (*Find factors and multiples*)
   To find the greatest number of groups, find the greatest common factor of 24, 48, and 304.

   Factors of 24: 1, 2, 3, 4, 6, 8, 12, 24

   Factors of 48: 1, 2, 3, 4, 6, 8, 12, 24, 48

   304 is not divisible by 48, 24, or 12, but it is divisible by 8 ($8 \times 38 = 304$), so 8 is the greatest common factor.

6. (continued)
   Incorrect choices:

   A 4 is a factor of all three numbers but is not the greatest common factor.

   C and **D** Both numbers are factors of 24 and 48, but not of 304.

7. Correct response: **C**
   (*Use expanded notation, exponents, and scientific notation*)
   Scientific notation represents the product of a decimal greater than or equal to 1 and less than 10 and a power of 10. 120,000 is $1.2 \times 10 \times 10 \times 10 \times 10 \times 10$, or 1.2×10^5. The exponent indicates the number of places to the right of the decimal point.

   Incorrect choices:

   A is not in scientific notation because "12" is not expressed as a decimal.

   B represents 12,000 (4 places to the right).

   D represents 1,200,000 (6 places to the right).

8. Correct response: **A**
   (*Use ratios to describe and compare two sets of data*)
   To find the ratio, compare the number of campers to counselors each year; for example, 18 to 3 in Year 1. The ratio of campers to counselors each year can be reduced to 6 to 1.

   Incorrect choices:

   B is the ratio of campers or counselors in the first year to the number of campers or counselors in the second year.

   C is the ratio of campers or counselors in the second year to the number of campers or counselors in the third year.

   D is the ratio of campers in the first year to the number of counselors in the fourth year.

9. Correct response: **A**
(*Add, subtract, multiply, and divide whole numbers*)

To find the number of tickets sold, divide the total cost of the tickets ($5,904) by the cost of each ticket ($12): $5,904 ÷ $12 = $492.

Incorrect choices:

B reflects an error in long division.

C reflects the sum of $5,904 and $12.

D reflects the product of $5,904 and $12.

10. Correct response: **B**
(*Add, subtract, multiply, and divide fractions and mixed numbers*)

To find the total number of acres, add $3\frac{2}{3}$ acres ($\frac{22}{6}$) + $2\frac{1}{6}$ acres ($\frac{13}{6}$), which equals $\frac{35}{6}$, or $5\frac{5}{6}$ acres.

Incorrect choices:

A reflects an error in adding $\frac{1}{6}$ and $\frac{2}{3}$, which does not equal $\frac{1}{2}$.

C reflects an error in adding $\frac{1}{6}$ and $\frac{2}{3}$, which does not equal 1.

D reflects the product of $3\frac{2}{3} \times 2\frac{1}{6}$.

11. Correct response: **A**
(*Add, subtract, multiply, and divide decimals*)

To find the difference in times between first place and second place, subtract: $48.21 - 46.69 = 1.52$ seconds.

Incorrect choices:

B, **C**, and **D** all reflect errors in subtracting decimals.

12. Correct response: **C**
(*Solve problems using ratios, rates, and proportions*)

According to the scale drawing, the house is 7 units high and 6 units wide, so the ratio of the height of the house to the width of the house is 7 to 6. If the height of the house is 28 feet, then an equation can be set up to find the width: $\frac{7}{28} = \frac{6}{x}$. Simplified, $x = 4(6) = 24$ feet.

12. (continued)
Incorrect choices:

A is the result of subtracting the height in the scale drawing (7) from the height of the house (28 feet).

B is the result of subtracting the width in the scale drawing (6) from the height of the house (28 feet).

D is the result of setting up an incorrect proportion ($\frac{7}{28} = \frac{x}{6}$) and multiplying the result times the height of the house (28 feet).

13. Correct response: **D**
(*Solve problems involving integers*)

To find the difference in temperature, subtract: $10°F - (-4°F)$, or $10°F + 4°F = 14°F$.

Incorrect choices:

A represents the number subtracted from $10°F: -(-4°F)$.

B reflects incorrect subtraction ($10°F - 4°F$).

C is the temperature on Monday.

14. Correct response: **C**
(*Estimate and round using whole numbers and decimals*)

The cost per pound can be rounded to $1.60, and the weight of Dexter's potatoes can be rounded to 3 pounds. The best estimate of the cost is $1.60 × 3 pounds = $4.80.

Incorrect choices:

A The cost of the potatoes is rounded down to $1.50 (× 3 = $4.50).

B The cost of the potatoes is rounded to $1.60 and added to 3 = $4.60.

D The cost of the potatoes is rounded up to $2 (× 3 = $6).

15. Correct response: **C**

(*Use order of operations to simplify whole number expressions*)

The problem should be solved in the following order:

1. Simplify inside the parentheses:
$6 + 4(8 - 4) \div 2 = 6 + 4(4) \div 2$

2. Multiply: $6 + 4(4) \div 2 = 6 + 16 \div 2$

3. Divide: $6 + 16 \div 2 = 6 + 8$

4. Add: $6 + 8 = 14$

Incorrect choices:

A is the result of dividing by 2 first: $6 + 2(4 - 2)$.

B is the result of adding before dividing in step 3: $22 \div 2$.

D is the result of adding first: $(6 + 4)[(8 - 4) \div 2]$.

16. Correct response: **A**

(*Apply the properties of operations*)

Matt and Selena's weights added together equal 187 pounds, and we know that Selena's weight is 85, so $85 + M = 187$. Addition and subtraction have an inverse relationship, so $187 - 85 = M$.

Incorrect choices:

B Adding the total weight and Selena's weight would not yield Matt's weight (addition does not have an inverse relationship with itself).

C The inverse equation has been set up incorrectly.

D The equation uses multiplication instead of addition.

17. Correct response: **B**

(*Solve multi-step problems involving whole numbers and fractions*)

After Amelia's picnic, there was 1 gallon $- \frac{2}{3}$ gallon of coffee ice cream, or $\frac{1}{3}$ gallon. After she and her parents ate another $\frac{1}{6}$ gallon, they had $\frac{1}{3}$ gallon $- \frac{1}{6}$ gallon $= \frac{1}{6}$ gallon left. $\frac{1}{6}$ gallon plus the $\frac{1}{2}$ gallon that her grandmother gave them $= \frac{1}{6} + \frac{1}{2}$, or $\frac{1}{6} + \frac{3}{6} = \frac{4}{6}$, or $\frac{2}{3}$ gallon.

Incorrect choices:

A is the result of $\frac{2}{3}$ gallon $+ \frac{1}{6}$ gallon $- \frac{1}{2}$ gallon.

C is the result of $\frac{2}{3}$ gallon $- \frac{1}{6}$ gallon $+ \frac{1}{2}$ gallon.

D is the result of $\frac{2}{3}$ gallon $+ \frac{1}{6}$ gallon $+ \frac{1}{2}$ gallon.

18. Correct response: **C**

(*Solve multi-step problems involving whole numbers*)

Rocky Point is a total of 140 miles + 30 miles = 170 miles from Canton. Deerfield is 90 miles from Rocky Point in the direction of Canton. Thus, it is 170 miles − 90 miles distant from Canton.

Incorrect choices:

A is the result of 140 miles − 30 miles − 90 miles.

B is the result of 140 miles − 90 miles.

D is the result of 140 miles + 30 miles + 90 miles.

19. Correct response: **B**

(*Convert or estimate conversions of metric measures*)

Since 1 meter = 100 centimeters, 1.6 meters $= 1.6 \times 100 = 160$ cm.

Incorrect choices:

A is the result of 1.6×10.

C is the result of $1.6 \times 1,000$.

D is the result of $1.6 \times 10,000$.

20. Correct response: **B**

(*Estimate and find length and perimeter*)

There are four equal sides to the square garden, so the length of fencing around (perimeter) will be 4 times the length of one side. The length of a side ($15\frac{5}{6}$ feet) can be rounded to 16 feet, and 16 feet × 4 feet = 64 feet.

Incorrect choices:

A is the result of rounding the length of each side to 15.

C equals the area of the garden if the length of each side is rounded to 15.

D equals the area of the garden if the length of each side is rounded to 16.

21. Correct response: **C**

(*Estimate and find length and perimeter*)

The perimeter of the triangle is the sum of its three sides. If two of the sides measure 25 feet each, then the third side is 90 ft − (25 ft + 25 ft) = 40 ft.

Incorrect choices:

A is the length of the base of a triangle with an area of 90 square feet and a height of 25 feet.

B assumes that the triangle is equilateral, so all three sides would measure 25 feet.

D is the result of subtracting 90 feet − 25 feet.

22. Correct response: **D**

(*Estimate and find surface area*)

The surface area of the box is the sum of the area of all of its sides:

2(1.5 ft × 3 ft) = 9 sq ft

2(2 ft × 3 ft) = 12 sq ft

2(1.5 ft × 2 ft) = 6 sq ft

9 sq ft + 12 sq ft + 6 sq ft = 27 sq ft

22. (continued)

Incorrect choices:

A is the volume of the box (3 ft × 2 ft × 1.5 ft).

B is the surface area for only half the box: (1.5 ft × 3 ft) + (1.5 ft × 2 ft) + (2 ft × 3 ft).

C is the surface area of the four long sides but not the ends: 2(1.5 ft × 3 ft) + 2(2 ft × 3 ft).

23. Correct response: **C**

(*Find area of a circle*)

If the diameter of the pool is 8 feet, then its radius is 8 feet ÷ 2 = 4 feet. The area is πr^2, or $\pi 4^2 = 16\pi$.

Incorrect choices:

A is π times 4 feet, the radius of the pool.

B is the circumference of the pool, or π times 8 feet.

D is π times the diameter squared instead of the radius squared.

24. Correct response: **A**

(*Find the sum of angles in simple polygons*)

The sum of the interior angles of a polygon is $(n - 2) \times 180°$, where n is the number of sides on the polygon. A pentagon has 5 sides, so $(5 - 2) \times 180° = 540°$.

Incorrect choices:

B is the result of $(n - 1) \times 180°$.

C is the result of $n \times 180°$.

D is the result of $(n + 2) \times 180°$.

25. Correct response: **D**

(*Estimate and measure angles*)

$\angle ABC$ is just slightly smaller than a straight angle (180°), so the best estimate of its measure is 160°.

Incorrect choices:

A represents an angle that is slightly smaller than a right angle.

B represents an angle that is slightly larger than a right angle.

C represents an angle that is about halfway between a right angle and a straight angle.

26. Correct response: **B**
(*Classify acute, obtuse, and right angles and triangles*)

An acute angle is less than 90°, and the angle shown in answer B is the only angle less than 90°.

Incorrect choices:

A is a right angle that measures exactly 90°.

C is an obtuse angle that measures more than 90°.

D is a straight angle that measures 180°.

27. Correct response: **A**
(*Identify, classify, and describe plane figures*)

A shape with four equal sides, two acute angles, and two obtuse angles is a parallelogram.

Incorrect choices:

B A square has four right angles, not two acute and two obtuse.

C A rectangle has four right angles, and the four sides do not all have to be equal.

D A trapezoid does not have four equal sides.

28. Correct response: **D**
(*Determine congruence and similarity of segments, angles, and polygons*)

The lengths of the sides of similar polygons are proportional. $\frac{6}{10} = \frac{3}{5}$, so the rectangle with sides of 3 and 5 is similar to the rectangle with sides of 6 and 10.

Incorrect choices:

A is not similar because $\frac{6}{20} \neq \frac{6}{10}$.

B is not similar because $\frac{4}{8} \neq \frac{6}{10}$.

C is not similar because $\frac{5}{12} \neq \frac{6}{10}$.

29. Correct response: **D**
(*Identify, classify, and describe solid figures*)

A square pyramid has a square base and four triangular sides.

29. (continued)
Incorrect choices:

A A rectangular prism has six sides, all of them rectangular.

B A triangular prism has two triangular sides and three rectangular sides.

C A triangular pyramid has a triangular base and three triangular sides.

30. Correct response: **B**
(*Locate and name points on a coordinate plane using ordered pairs*)

Point *A* is located at (6, 3) on the coordinate grid. To find the point that is 3 squares to the right and 2 units down, add 3 to the *x* value ($6 + 3 = 9$) and subtract 2 from the *y* value ($3 - 2 = 1$). The point will be at (9, 1).

Incorrect choices:

A reverses the *x*- and *y*-coordinates.

C is the result of moving 3 squares down and 2 squares right.

D is the result of moving 3 squares to the left and 2 squares down.

31. Correct response: **C**
(*Locate and name points on a coordinate plane using ordered pairs*)

To find the point that is halfway between *M* and *N*, find the *x*-value that is halfway between the *x*-coordinates of the points and the *y*-coordinates that is halfway between the *y*-coordinates of the two points. Point *M* is at (4, 2) and point *N* is at (8, 8). The *x*-value halfway between 4 and 8 is 6, and the *y*-value halfway between 2 and 8 is 5. The halfway point is located at (6, 5).

Incorrect choices:

A and **D** represent other points on the grid resulting from guesses or incorrect calculations to find the midpoint between *M* and *N*.

B reverses the *x*- and *y*-coordinates.

32. Correct response: **B**
(*Identify and describe points, lines, planes, and relationships among them*)

The two line segments are parallel because they intersect two parallel lines at congruent angles.

32. (continued)
Incorrect choices:

A and **C** are incorrect because the lines do not intersect each other and cannot be perpendicular.

D is incorrect because the term "complementary" does not describe two lines.

33. Correct response: **D**
(*Transform figures in the coordinate plane*)
Point A is located at $(1, 3)$. If $\triangle ABC$ is reflected across the line $x = 4$, the y-coordinate of point A will remain the same. The x-coordinate will be an equal distance from $x = 4$ on the opposite side. Three units greater than 4 is 7. The coordinates of point A will be $(7, 3)$.

Incorrect choices:

A is the result of a translation to the other side of $x = 4$.

B is the result of reflecting the triangle incorrectly.

C is the result of a translation to the other side of $x = 4$ and switching the x- and y-coordinates.

34. Correct response: **A**
(*Solve problems involving length*)
The total amount of fencing will be the perimeter of the ranch (14.6 km) plus the perimeter of the corral. The corral is a square with sides of 65 meters, so its perimeter is 4×65 m $= 260$ m, or 0.260 km. 14.6 km $+ 0.260$ km $= 14.86$ km.

Incorrect choices:

B is the sum of 14.6 km $+ 2.6$ km (the decimal is misplaced when converting meters to kilometers).

C is the sum of 14.6 km plus the area of the corral (65 m $\times$ 65 m $= 4.225$ km^2).

D is the sum of 14.6 km $+ 65$ km, which is only one side of the corral.

35. Correct response: **B**
(*Solve problems involving time*)
The total time the plane spends between Detroit and New York City is 4 hours 28 minutes, plus 2 hours 7 minutes, plus 2 hours 55 minutes, or a total of 9 hours 30 minutes. If the plane leaves Detroit at 7:15 A.M. and arrives in New York City 9 hours 30 minutes later, it will arrive at 4:45 P.M.

Incorrect choices:

A is the result of adding the times as decimals instead of minutes ($4.28 + 2.32 + 2.55 = 9.15$; $7:15 + 9.15$ hour $= 4:30$ P.M.).

C is the result of adding the times as decimals instead of minutes and does not account for the 12-hour time cycle ($7:15 + 9.15 = 16.30$, which would be 6:30 P.M.).

D reflects an error in calculation, adding an extra hour to the time.

36. Correct response: **C**
(*Match 3-dimensional objects and their 2-dimensional representations*)
The net shown in choice C can be folded to make a cube.

Incorrect responses:

A, **B**, and **D** cannot be folded to make cubes. (This can be demonstrated by cutting and folding nets like these from separate paper.)

37. Correct response: **A**
(*Interpret data presented in a circle graph*)
Just under half of the students are from Georgetown, while just over a quarter of the students are from Montgomery and Watertown combined.

Incorrect choices:

B There are slightly fewer students from Rivervale than from Montgomery and Watertown combined.

C There are fewer students from Georgetown than from all of the other schools combined.

D Fewer than half of the students come from Georgetown.

38. Correct response: **C**
(*Interpret data presented in a circle graph*)
   Hummus and peanut butter and jelly each represent about a quarter of the sales, so together they make up about half of the sales.

Incorrect choices:

A Turkey sandwiches represent less than half of the sales.

B Sam's sold about the same number of peanut butter and jelly sandwiches and hummus sandwiches.

D Although Sam's sold more turkey sandwiches than any other one kind of sandwich, turkey sandwiches still made up less than half of the sales.

39. Correct response: **D**
(*Interpret data in a stem-and-leaf plot*)
   The number of students who scored at least an 80 on the test is the total number of leaves following the stems of 8 and 9, which represent 80 and 90 respectively. There are 7 students who scored in the 80's and 8 students who scored in the 90's, for a total of 15 students with a score of at least 80.

Incorrect choices:

A is the number of stems.

B is the number of students who scored from 80 to 89.

C is the number of students who scored from 90 to 99.

40. Correct response: **C**
(*Find permutations and combinations*)
   The number of permutations is the number of possible choices for the first time Crystal draws a tile (26) times the number of possible choices for the second time Crystal chooses a tile (25). $26 \times 25 = 650$.

Incorrect choices:

A is the sum of $25 + 26$.

B is the number of possible combinations (the same two tiles in different order).

D is the number of permutations if Crystal had replaced the first tile (26×26).

41. Correct response: **B**
(*Find probabilities*)
   Since each number cube could land on one of 6 sides, there are $6 \times 6 = 36$ possible results. There are 6 ways that the cubes could land on the same number (1 and 1, 2 and 2, and so on). Therefore, the probability that they will land on the same number is $\frac{6}{36} = \frac{1}{6}$.

Incorrect choices:

A is the result of $\frac{6}{(6 + 6)}$.

C is the result of $\frac{1}{(6 + 6)}$.

D is the result of $\frac{1}{(6 \times 6)}$.

42. Correct response: **D**
(*Determine and compare experimental and theoretical probabilities for simple and compound events, independent and dependent events*)
   The experimental probability that the coin will land on heads is based on the outcomes of the previous experiments. In Rachel's experiment, the coin landed on heads 7 out of 10 times, or 70% of the time, so the experimental probability is 70%.

Incorrect choices:

A 50% is the theoretical probability, not the experimental.

B The experimental probability is 70% and the theoretical probability is 50%.

C reflects a misunderstanding of how to calculate theoretical probability.

43. Correct response: **A**
(*Determine and describe the mean, median, mode, and range of data*)
   To find the mean, add the heights of all the trees (342 ft) and divide by the number of trees (9). The mean height is 342 ft ÷ 9 = 38 ft.

Incorrect choices:

B is the median height.

C is the mode of the data.

D is the total of all the heights.

44. Correct response: **A**

(*Determine and describe the mean, median, mode, and range of data*)

   The mode is the response given most often. Seven students had 3 cousins, which is more responses than any of the other numbers of cousins.

Incorrect choices:

B is the median number of cousins.

C is the "middle bar" and reflects a misconception of how to figure the median from a bar graph.

D is the number of respondents who had 3 cousins.

45. Correct response: **B**

(*Collect, organize, display, and interpret data to solve problems*)

   Since 14 students plan to vote for Aditri, and 8 students plan to vote for Casey, the difference is $14 - 8 = 6$.

Incorrect choices:

A is the result of misreading the numbers on the vertical axis, assuming that each square equals 1 vote instead of 2 ($7 - 4 = 3$).

C is the number of students planning to vote for Casey.

D is the number of students planning to vote for Aditri.

46. Correct response: **C**

(*Identify, describe, and extend geometric patterns*)

   The total number of stairs in the staircase is the sum of the number of blocks in each step. Since each step increases by one block, the total number of blocks in the stairs are triangular numbers. When the highest stair has 10 blocks, the total number of blocks will be $1 + 2 + 3 + 4 + 5 + 6 + 7 + 8 + 9 + 10 = 55$.

Incorrect choices:

A is the sum of 6 blocks + 10 blocks.

B is the number of blocks in a staircase with 9 blocks in the highest step.

D is the product of 6×10.

47. Correct response: **A**

(*Interpret, write, and simplify algebraic expressions*)

   If m represents the number of 6-foot pieces and n represents the number of 2-foot pieces of rope, then $6m$ is the total length of the 6-foot pieces and $2n$ is the total length of the 2-foot pieces. The sum of those lengths ($6m + 2n$) is the total length of rope, 200 feet.

Incorrect choices:

B subtracts the 2-foot pieces from the 6-foot pieces.

C multiplies the 6-foot and 2-foot pieces.

D divides the total length by 6-foot pieces.

48. Correct response: **A**

(*Apply basic properties and order of operations with algebraic expressions*)

   Using the distributive property, $4 + 3(a + b) = 4 + 3a + 3b$.

Incorrect choices:

B is the result of multiplying a and b instead of adding.

C represents a misunderstanding of the distributive property.

D is the result of adding $4 + 3$ before distributing 3 across ($a + b$).

49. Correct response: **C**

(*Model, represent, and solve mathematical relationships with graphs using words or symbols*)

   Choice C is the graphical representation of the line $y = 2x$; every point on the line satisfies this equation.

Incorrect choices:

A shows the graph of line $y = x$.

B shows the graph of line $y = x + 2$.

D shows the graph of line $y = \frac{x}{2}$.

50. Correct response: **A**

(*Solve one-step and two-step linear equations*)

To solve for x, first multiply both sides by x:

$$\frac{36}{x}(x) = 4(x)$$

$$36 = 4x$$

Then divide both sides by 4 to get the answer $x = 9$.

Incorrect choices:

B is the result of subtracting $36 - 4$.

C is the result of adding $36 + 4$.

D is the result of multiplying 36×4.

51. Correct response: **D**

(*Solve simple one-step and two-step inequalities*)

To solve the inequality, subtract 27 from both sides:

$$s + 27 - 27 \leq 40 - 27$$

$$s \leq 13$$

Incorrect choices:

A is the result of adding 27 to 40 and flipping the inequality sign.

B is the result of adding 27 to 40.

C flips the inequality sign.

52. Correct response: **B**

(*Represent linear functions using graphs*)

The graph in choice B shows the line $y = x + 3$ ($x \geq 0$).

Incorrect choices:

A shows the graph of the line $y = x - 3$ ($x \geq 0$).

C shows the graph of the line $y = 3x$ ($x \geq 0$).

D shows the graph of the line $y = 3$ ($x \geq 0$).

53. Correct response: **C**

(*Make conjectures, predictions, and generalizations from patterns, data, or examples*)

Jorge's average has increased by 4–6% each year, while Warren's average has improved by only 2–3% each year.

Incorrect choices:

A is valid only for the first three years.

B is valid only for the last two years.

D is incorrect because Jorge's average has increased more quickly.

54. Correct response: **B**

(*Evaluate the reasonableness of a solution*)

One way to determine whether a solution is reasonable is to round the numbers in the problem to determine the appropriate number of digits in the solution. The diameter of the crater is approximately 8,000 ft, and π is approximately 3. The circumference of a circle can be found with the formula $C = \pi d$, so $8{,}000 \times 3 = 24{,}000$. The most reasonable solution will have five digits.

Incorrect choices:

A is not reasonable because it is even less than the diameter of 8,145 ft.

C and **D** both have more digits than is reasonable for solutions to the problem.

Test ② Answer Key

1. B	**12.** D	**23.** B	**34.** B	**45.** B
2. B	**13.** B	**24.** A	**35.** A	**46.** D
3. A	**14.** C	**25.** C	**36.** A	**47.** D
4. C	**15.** B	**26.** B	**37.** B	**48.** A
5. D	**16.** D	**27.** A	**38.** C	**49.** B
6. C	**17.** C	**28.** B	**39.** A	**50.** B
7. B	**18.** A	**29.** D	**40.** D	**51.** D
8. B	**19.** D	**30.** A	**41.** B	**52.** C
9. D	**20.** D	**31.** C	**42.** A	**53.** A
10. D	**21.** B	**32.** A	**43.** B	**54.** C
11. C	**22.** C	**33.** C	**44.** C	

Answer Key Explanations

1. Correct response: **B**
(*Compare and order fractions and decimals*)
0.6 is equal to $\frac{6}{10}$, or $\frac{12}{20}$, which is greater than $\frac{8}{20}$.

Incorrect choices:

A reflects an error in ordering fractions; it assumes that $\frac{6}{10} < \frac{6}{12}$, but the opposite is true.

C reflects a misconception about how to order decimals, since 0.63 is greater than 0.6.

D is incorrect because $0.6 = \frac{6}{10}$, not $\frac{10}{6}$; the numerator and denominator have been reversed.

2. Correct response: **B**
(*Compare, order, and use percents*)
To find the 15% tip, multiply $22 × 0.15. The tip will be $3.30. The sum of $22 + $3.30 is $25.30. To find the amount she should keep out of $40, subtract: $40 − $25.30 = $14.70.

2. (continued)
Incorrect choices:

A is the amount of the tip.

C is the result of figuring the tip incorrectly before subtracting (it assumes that a 15% tip is $1.50).

D is the total cost of the meal plus tip; this is the amount that Juno will pay.

3. Correct response: **A**
(*Compare, order, and use integers*)
The higher the absolute value of a negative integer, the smaller it is. Thus, −5 is less than −4.

Incorrect choices:

B disregards the negative signs; −5 is greater than −6.

C represents a misconception about negative integers.

D also represents a misconception since the negative integer (−5) is less than the positive integer (3).

4. Correct response: **C**
(*Identify and use place value*)

One million is a 1 followed by six zeros; the millions place has six digits following it before the decimal point. In the number 25,731,000, the **5** is in the millions place; it has six digits to the right.

Incorrect choices:

A 2 is in the ten millions place.

B 3 is in the thousands place.

D 7 is in the hundred thousands place.

5. Correct response: **D**
(*Identify and describe prime and composite numbers, and prime factors*)

The ninth grade has 123 students, which is a composite number ($123 = 3 \times 41$), so this number can be divided evenly into more than one group.

Incorrect choices:

A, **B**, and **C** are incorrect because the numbers 109, 113, and 137 are all prime numbers and cannot be evenly divided.

6. Correct response: **C**
(*Find factors and multiples*)

Multiples of 12 include 12, 24, 48, 60, 72, 84, 96, 108. Multiples of 32 include 32, 64, 96, 128, 160. So the least common multiple for these numbers is 96.

Incorrect choices:

A 12 is one factor; it is not a multiple of 32.

B 64 is a multiple of 32 but is not a multiple of 12.

D 384 is a common multiple of 12 and 32 but not the least common multiple.

7. Correct response: **B**
(*Use expanded notation, exponents, and scientific notation*)

625 is 5^4, which is written as $5 \times 5 \times 5 \times 5$ in expanded form.

7. (continued)
 Incorrect choices:

A is written in scientific notation.

C is not written in expanded form; 25 is not a prime number.

D has too many factors; $5 \times 5 \times 5 \times 5 \times 5 = 3{,}125$.

8. Correct response: **B**
(*Use ratios to describe and compare two sets of data*)

The ratio of angelfish to goldfish in each set (3 to 12, 5 to 20, and 8 to 32) can be reduced to 1 to 4.

Incorrect choices:

A is the difference between the number of goldfish and angelfish (9) compared to Group 1.

C is the ratio of angelfish in the first set (3) to the number of angelfish in the second set (5).

D is the ratio of angelfish in the first set (3) to the number of goldfish in the third set (32).

9. Correct response: **D**
(*Add, subtract, multiply, and divide whole numbers*)

The number of cookies baked in a normal day is 3 dozen (3×12) $\times$ 365 days, or 13,140.

Incorrect choices:

A is the product of 3×365.

B reflects an error in multiplication or the size of a dozen: $(3 \times 3) \times 365$.

C is the product of 12×365 days.

10. Correct response: **D**
(*Add, subtract, multiply, and divide fractions*)

The number of test tubes that can be filled is the number of liters of acid divided by the capacity of one test tube: $\frac{8}{5} \div \frac{1}{8}$, or $\frac{8}{5} \times \frac{8}{1} = \frac{64}{5}$, or $12\frac{4}{5}$.

10. (continued)
Incorrect choices:

A is the product of $\frac{8}{5} \times \frac{1}{8}$.

B is the difference between $\frac{8}{5}$ and $\frac{1}{8}$.

C is the inverse of $\frac{8}{5} \times \frac{1}{8}$.

11. Correct response: **C**
(*Add, subtract, multiply, and divide decimals*)
The number of batches of biscuits the baker can make is the amount of flour in the sack divided by the amount of flour it takes to make a batch of biscuits: $6.28 \text{ kg} \div 0.4 \text{ kg} = 15.7$ batches.

Incorrect choices:

A and **D** both reflect incorrect placement of the decimal when dividing.

B is the result of multiplying 6.28 by 0.4 instead of dividing.

12. Correct response: **D**
(*Solve problems using ratios, rates, and proportions*)
If Emiko walks 3 miles in 45 minutes, then she walks 1 mile in 15 minutes $(45 \div 3)$. At 15 minutes per mile, Emiko will take $15 \times 5 = 75$ minutes to walk 5 miles. Expressed as a proportion, this problem can be solved using the equation $\frac{3}{45} = \frac{5}{x}$.

Incorrect choices:

A is the result of setting up an incorrect proportion $(\frac{5}{45} = \frac{3}{x})$.

B is the sum of $45 + (3 \times 5)$

C is the result of incorrectly identifying the time to walk one mile as 9 minutes $(45 \div 5)$, and then adding the time for an extra two miles of walking (18 minutes) to 45 minutes.

13. Correct response: **B**
(*Solve problems involving integers*)
The change in temperature is $-12°C - (-7°C)$, or $-12°C + 7°C = -5°C$.

13. (continued)
Incorrect choices:

A is the result of adding $-7°C + (-12°C)$.

C is the result of subtracting $12°C - 7°C$ without regard for the negative signs.

D is the result of adding $7°C + 12°C$.

14. Correct response: **C**
(*Estimate and round using whole numbers*)
The miles remaining are equal to the total distance of 1,504 (which can be rounded to 1,500) minus the miles already driven (which can be rounded to $500 + 500$, or 1,000): $1,500 - 1,000 = 500$.

Incorrect choices:

A reflects an error in subtracting.

B is the result of $1,500 - (600 + 500)$.

D is the result of $1,500 - (400 + 500)$.

15. Correct response: **B**
(*Use order of operations to simplify whole-number expressions*)
The problem should be solved in the following order:

1. Simplify inside the parentheses:
$2 + (3 + 3)^2 \div 4 - 1 = 2 + 6^2 \div 4 - 1$

2. Simplify the exponent: $2 + 6^2 \div 4 - 1 = 2 + 36 \div 4 - 1$

3. Divide: $2 + (36 \div 4) - 1 = 2 + 9 - 1$

4. Add and subtract from left to right:
$2 + 9 - 1 = 10$

Incorrect choices:

A is the result of simplifying from left to right after step 2: $(2 + 36) \div 4 - 1$.

C is the result of adding and subtracting before dividing in step 3: $(2 + 36) \div (4 - 1)$.

D is the result of simplifying from left to right: $(2 + 3 + 3)^2 \div 4 - 1$.

16. Correct response: **D**
(*Apply the properties of operations*)

In this problem, Jake's equation expresses the amount of money as repeated addition; it can also be expressed as multiplication (5×6).

Incorrect choices:

A represents $5 \times 5 \times 5 \times 5 \times 5 \times 5$.

B represents 5×5.

C represents $6 \times 6 \times 6 \times 6 \times 6$.

17. Correct response: **C**
(*Solve multi-step problems involving whole numbers*)

Jill divides the 52 cards evenly among the 4 players, so each player has $52 \div 4 = 13$ cards. Misha gives Jill 2 cards on his turn, so Jill has $13 + 2 = 15$ cards. Then Jill gives Charese 3 cards on her turn, so she has $15 - 3 = 12$ cards.

Incorrect choices:

A is the result of subtracting cards on both turns: $52 \div 4 - 2 - 3$.

B is the result of subtracting 3 cards given to Charese but not adding 2 cards she received: $52 \div 4 - 3$.

D is the result of adding 3 cards and subtracting 2: $52 \div 4 + 3 - 2$.

18. Correct response: **A**
(*Solve multi-step problems involving whole numbers and decimals*)

The building is divided into 20 equal stories, so each story is $64 \text{ m} \div 20 = 3.2 \text{ m}$ tall. The height from floor to ceiling of each story is the height of the story minus the space left for pipes and the thickness of the floor, or $3.2 \text{ m} - 0.7 \text{ m} - 0.14 \text{ m} = 2.36 \text{ m}$.

Incorrect choices:

B is the result of subtracting the thickness of the floor and adding the space left for pipes: $3.2 - 0.7 + 0.14$.

C is the result of an error in placing the decimal point before subtracting: $3.2 - 0.07 - 0.14$.

D is the result of adding the thickness of the floor and the space left for pipes: $3.2 + 0.7 + 0.14$.

19. Correct response: **D**
(*Convert or estimate conversions of measures*)

One gallon is approximately 4 liters (1 gallon = 3.79 L), so a 6-gallon bucket holds approximately $6 \times 4 \text{ L} = 24 \text{ L}$ of water.

Incorrect choices:

A is the result of reversing the conversion $(6 \div 4$ instead of $6 \times 4)$.

B assumes a 1-to-1 ratio of gallons to liters.

C is the result of assuming that 1 gallon equals about 3 liters: $6 \times 3 = 18$.

20. Correct response: **D**
(*Estimate and find length and perimeter*)

The perimeter is $(2 \times \text{length}) + (2 \times \text{width})$, or $2l + 2w$. The length of the mirror is 6 ft and the width is 2 ft, so $2(6 \text{ ft}) + 2(2 \text{ ft}) = 16 \text{ ft}$.

Incorrect choices:

A is the length of the mirror.

B is the length plus the width.

C is the area of the mirror $(6 \text{ ft} \times 2 \text{ ft})$.

21. Correct response: **B**
(*Estimate and find length and area*)

To find the length of the field, divide the area by the width. The area can be rounded to 500, and the width can be rounded to 20; $500 \div 20 = 25$.

Incorrect choices:

A is the result of rounding the area down to 400; $400 \div 20 = 20$.

C would be the approximate length of the playground if 494 were the perimeter instead of the area.

D is the result of multiplying 500×20 instead of dividing.

22. Correct response: **C**
(*Estimate and find volume/capacity*)

The volume of the box is its height $\times$ width $\times$ length, or $10 \text{ cm} \times 4 \text{ cm} \times 4 \text{ cm} = 160 \text{ cm}^3$.

22. (continued)

Incorrect choices:

A is the sum of the height, width, and length (4 + 4 + 10).

B is the product of the height × length (4 × 10).

D is the surface area of the box, rather than its volume.

23. Correct response: **B**

(*Find circumference of a circle*)

The amount of fencing will be the circumference of the play area, or π times the diameter of the circle. The diameter is 20 m, so the circumference is 20π m.

Incorrect choices:

A is π times the radius of the play area instead of its diameter.

C is the area of the play area (π × 10²).

D is π times the diameter squared.

24. Correct response: **A**

(*Estimate and measure angles*)

Use a protractor to find that the measure of ∠NOP is 73°. To use the protractor correctly, line segment OP should be lined up with 0°.

Incorrect choices:

B is a slightly incorrect measurement.

C is the result of reading the protractor from 180° backward instead of from 0° forward.

D is the result of lining up line segment OP with 90°.

25. Correct response: **C**

(*Classify acute, obtuse, and right angles and triangles*)

An obtuse triangle has one angle that is greater than 90°.

Incorrect choices:

A is an acute triangle, having three angles less than 90°.

B is a right triangle, having one right angle.

D is an equilateral triangle with three acute angles.

26. Correct response: **B**

(*Identify, classify, and describe plane figures*)

A trapezoid is a four-sided figure with one set of parallel sides.

Incorrect choices:

A describes an isosceles triangle.

C describes a pentagon.

D describes a parallelogram.

27. Correct response: **A**

(*Determine congruence and similarity of segments, angles, and polygons*)

Since quadrilateral ABCD is a square, its diagonals bisect each other. Therefore, $\overline{AE}$ is congruent to $\overline{EC}$.

Incorrect choices:

B and **D** are sides of the square ($\overline{AD}$ and $\overline{CD}$), which are not equal to half the diagonal.

C is the full diagonal ($\overline{BD}$), which is twice the length of $\overline{EC}$.

28. Correct response: **B**

(*Identify, classify, and describe solid figures*)

A triangular pyramid has 4 faces, and a rectangular prism has 6 faces: 6 − 4 = 2.

Incorrect choices:

A, **C**, and **D** all reflect mistakes in determining the number of faces these figures have.

29. Correct response: **D**

(*Locate and name points on a coordinate plane using ordered pairs*)

The shaded figure has vertices at points (2, 2), (2, 7), (6, 2), and (6, 9).

Incorrect choices:

A The coordinates in the third and fourth ordered pairs have been reversed.

B The coordinates in the second and fourth ordered pairs have been reversed.

C The coordinates in the second, third, and fourth ordered pairs have been reversed.

30. Correct response: **A**
(*Locate and name points on a coordinate plane using ordered pairs*)
    The center point of the fountain will be located at the center of the rectangle, which is at point (5, 4).

Incorrect choices:

B is the center point of one side of the rectangle.

C reverses the *x*- and *y*-coordinates.

D is the center point of one side of the rectangle.

31. Correct response: **C**
(*Identify and describe points, lines, planes, and relationships among them*)
    Oak St. and Center St. intersect at a 90° angle, making them perpendicular.

Incorrect choices:

A and **B** name streets that intersect, but not at 90° angles.

D Oak Street and Main Street are parallel.

32. Correct response: **A**
(*Transform figures in the coordinate plane*)
    The location of point B is (3, 6). If it is translated 2 units to the right, then the *x*-value will increase by 2. The location of point *B* after the translation will be (5, 6).

Incorrect choices:

B is the location of point *C* after the translation.

C is the location of point *B* if it were translated 2 units to the left.

D is the location of point *B* if it were reflected over the line *y* = 5.

33. Correct response: **C**
(*Solve problems involving weight*)
    The amount of weight that the puppy gained during its first year is its weight at the end of the year (6 lb 4 oz) minus its weight at birth (5.5 oz). 6 lb 4 oz − 5.5 oz = 5 lb 14.5 oz.

33. (continued)
Incorrect choices:

A is the result of changing 6 lb 4 oz to 6.4 and subtracting: 6.4 − 5.5.

B would be correct if there were 10 ounces to a pound.

D is the result of adding 6 lb 4 oz + 5.5 oz.

34. Correct response: **B**
(*Solve problems involving temperature and time*)
    The amount that the temperature increased each hour is the total increase in temperature (27°) divided by the total number of hours (10:00 to 4:00 = 6 hours): 27°F ÷ 6 hr = 4.5°F per hour.

Incorrect choices:

A is the result of an error in division.

C is the result of dividing 27° by 5 hours.

D is the result of dividing 27° by 4 hours.

35. Correct response: **A**
(*Match 3-dimensional objects and their 2-dimensional representations*)
    From above, the wall will appear to be a rectangle. Drawing with perspective often makes rectangles look like triangles as the shape recedes into the distance.

Incorrect choices:

B, **C**, and **D** reflect misunderstandings of perspective drawings.

36. Correct response: **A**
(*Interpret data presented in a line graph*)
    Alfredo's sold the most spaghetti in January (about 670 pounds). The data point for January is the highest point on the line graph.

Incorrect choices:

B February's sales (550 lbs) were lower than January's.

C Alfredo's sold less spaghetti in March (300 lbs) than in January.

D represents the month with the second-highest sales (600 lbs).

37. Correct response: **B**

(*Interpret data presented in a line graph*)

The period of greatest decrease was February to March: 550 lbs to 300 lbs. This was a decrease of 250 lbs (550 lbs − 300 lbs).

Incorrect choices:

A Alfredo's spaghetti sales decreased more between February and March. The decrease from January to February was 670 − 550 = 120 lbs.

C The decrease from April to May (600 − 425 = 175 lbs) was less than the decrease from February to March.

D Alfredo's spaghetti sales were at their lowest in June, but the decrease from May to June (425 − 225 = 200 lbs) was less than in February to March.

38. Correct response: **C**

(*Interpret data in a line plot*)

The number of players who are at least 65 inches tall is the total number of X's that are stacked above the 65 inches mark plus all of the heights greater than 65 inches. There are a total of 12 X's that satisfy these conditions.

Incorrect choices:

A is the number of players who are exactly 65 inches tall; the question asks for the number of players who are *at least* 65 inches.

B is the number of players who are more than 65 inches tall.

D is the number of players who are 65 inches tall or less (from 59 in. to 65 in.).

39. Correct response: **A**

(*Construct sample spaces using lists, charts, frequency tables, and tree diagrams*)

The tree diagram should show a single path for every possible combination of one sweatshirt and one pair of shorts. Jill has 3 sweatshirts and can wear any of 3 pairs of shorts with each sweatshirt, so there are 9 possible combinations (3 × 3) and 9 paths in the diagram.

39. (continued)

Incorrect choices:

B shows only 3 of the 9 possible combinations.

C and **D** are constructed incorrectly.

40. Correct response: **D**

(*Find permutations and combinations*)

To find the number of possible combinations, use the fundamental counting principle: multiply the number of ways each event can occur. There are 4 choices of ice cream flavors, 4 choices of topping, and 2 choices of sauce: 4 × 4 × 2 = 32.

Incorrect choices:

A is the result of adding 4 + 4 + 2 instead of multiplying.

B is the result of (4 + 4) × 2 or 4 × 4.

C is the result of miscounting the number of toppings and multiplying 4 × 3 × 2.

41. Correct response: **B**

(*Find probabilities*)

There are a total of 24 gumballs in the machine (8 + 4 + 3 + 9), and 8 of them are red. The probability that a customer will choose a red gumball is $\frac{8}{24} = \frac{1}{3}$.

Incorrect choices:

A is the result of figuring 8 red gumballs and 16 other colors: $\frac{8}{16} = \frac{1}{2}$.

C is the probability that the gumball will be yellow ($\frac{4}{24} = \frac{1}{6}$).

D is the probability that the gumball will be green ($\frac{3}{24} = \frac{1}{8}$), or it could represent the fraction 1 over the number of red gumballs.

42. Correct response: **A**
(*Determine and compare experimental and theoretical probabilities for simple and compound events, independent and dependent events*)

The probability of picking a blue marble from the bag of 10 marbles is $\frac{3}{10}$. The probability of picking a blue marble from the box of 8 marbles is $\frac{5}{8}$. The probability of picking a blue marble from both the bag and the box is $\frac{3}{10} \times \frac{5}{8} = \frac{15}{80}$, or $\frac{3}{16}$.

Incorrect choices:

B is the total number of blue marbles ($3 + 5 = 8$) divided by the total number of yellow marbles ($3 + 7 = 10$).

C is the result of determining the individual probabilities incorrectly: $\frac{3}{7} \times \frac{5}{3}$.

D is the probability of choosing a blue marble from either the bag or the box: $\frac{3}{10} + \frac{5}{8} = \frac{37}{40}$.

43. Correct response: **B**
(*Determine and describe the mean, median, mode, and range of data*)

The range is the difference between the highest temperature ($65°$) and the lowest temperature ($60°$) in the table: $65° - 60° = 5°$.

Incorrect choices:

A is the difference between the first temperature listed ($62°$) and the last temperature listed ($63°$).

C is the mode of these data; $61°$ appears more often than any other temperature.

D is the highest temperature listed in the table.

44. Correct response: **C**
(*Determine and describe the mean, median, mode, and range of data*)

To find the median, put all of the prices in order and find the middle price. Since there are 12 pairs of shoes, there are two middle values (125 and 129). The mean of these numbers—or the number halfway between them—is the median: $\frac{125 + 129}{2} = 127$.

44. (continued)
Incorrect choices:

A is the range of values ($310 - 65 = 245$).

B is the mean value of all the prices ($1{,}740 \div 12$ prices $= 145$).

D is the 6th price value in order, mistaken for the median.

45. Correct response: **B**
(*Collect, organize, display, and interpret data to solve problems*)

The number of students who voted for blue can be determined by multiplying $600 \times 0.35 = 210$. The number of students who voted for yellow is $600 \times 0.10 = 60$. The difference between these numbers is $210 - 60 = 150$.

Incorrect choices:

A is the difference between the percentages of students who voted for blue (35%) and yellow (10%): $35 - 10 = 25$.

C is the number of students who voted for blue: $600 \times 0.35 = 210$.

D is 600 minus the difference of the percentages of students who voted for blue and yellow ($35 - 10 = 25$): $600 - 25 = 575$.

46. Correct response: **D**
(*Identify, describe, and extend numerical patterns*)

Each year, Flora's allowance grows by $4, which means that it is growing by a factor of 4. Therefore, $4n$ will be part of the expression that describes the pattern, where n represents the year. The expression that describes the relationship between each year and Flora's allowance is $4n + 1$ ($4 per year $+ 1$ year).

Incorrect choices:

A describes only the relationship between Flora's allowance ($4) and Year 1.

B describes only the relationship between Flora's allowance and Year 2.

C describes only the relationship between Flora's allowance and Year 3.

47. Correct response: **D**
(*Interpret, write, and simplify algebraic expressions*)

To simplify the equation, combine like terms: $(-4x^2 + 6x^2) + 10x + (4 + 8) = 2x^2 + 10x + 12$.

Incorrect choices:

A is the result of adding all of the coefficients $(10 + 4 - 4 + 8 + 6 = 24)$ and putting them in front of the greatest power of x.

B is the result of combining the x and x^2 terms $(10x + 4x^2 + 6x^2)$.

C is the result of adding $10x + 4 + 4x^2 + 8 + 6x^2$.

48. Correct response: **A**
(*Apply basic properties and order of operations with algebraic expressions*)

Using the commutative property, $q \times (p + 2) = q \times (2 + p)$

Incorrect choices:

B, **C**, and **D** all represent misunderstandings of the basic properties.

49. Correct response: **B**
(*Model, represent, and solve mathematical relationships with tables, graphs, and rules using words or symbols*)

Based on the other values in the table, the output is 5 times the input $(2 \times 5 = 10, 5 \times 5 = 25, 8 \times 5 = 40)$. To apply this rule and to find the input n for an output of 35, divide 35 by 5: $35 \div 5 = 7$.

Incorrect choices:

A represents an error in calculation or the use of the factor 5 instead of 7: $35 \div 7 = 5$.

C represents a misunderstanding of the input-output table, adding 3 to the previous input $(2 + 3 = 5, 5 + 3 = 8, 8 + 3 = 11)$.

D represents a misunderstanding of the input-output table, adding 5 to the previous input $(8 + 5 = 13)$.

50. Correct response: **B**
(*Solve one-step and two-step linear equations*)

To solve for w, first add 3 to each side:

$$4w - 3 + 3 = 11 + 3$$

$$4w = 14$$

Then divide each side by 4 to get the answer $w = 3.5$.

Incorrect responses:

A is the result of subtracting 3 from 11 instead of adding $(4w = 11 - 3)$.

C is the result of subtracting 3 from 11 instead of adding $(4w = 11 - 3)$ and multiplying 8 by 4 instead of dividing $(w = 8 \times 4)$.

D is the result of multiplying 14 by 4 instead of dividing $(w = 14 \times 4)$.

51. Correct response: **D**
(*Solve simple one-step and two-step inequalities*)

To solve the inequality, first subtract 140 from both sides:

$$140 + 5b - 140 \geq 500 - 140$$

$$5b \geq 360$$

Then divide both sides by 5 to get the answer: $b \geq 72$.

Incorrect choices:

A is the result of adding 140 to 500 and flipping the inequality sign.

B is the result of adding 140 to 500.

C is the result of flipping the inequality sign.

52. Correct response: **C**
(*Represent linear functions using tables, equations, and graphs*)

For each time shown on the table, the distance traveled is half as great (for example, 2 minutes and 1 mile). Therefore, the distance (d) $= \frac{1}{2}$ the time (t).

52. (continued)

Incorrect choices:

A represents only the first set of values $(2 - 1)$.

B represents a reversal of the third set of values, where $t = d + 3$.

D represents a reversal of distance and time values (in the table, each t value $= 2d$).

53. Correct response: **A**
(*Make conjectures, predictions, and generalizations from patterns, data, or examples*)

The ticket sales are decreasing by about 100 tickets per week. The theater sold about 400 tickets in week 6. In week 8, the ticket sales would be expected to fall by another 200 tickets. $400 - 200 = 200$.

Incorrect choices:

B would be a good prediction of ticket sales for week 7.

C is approximately the ticket sales for week 6.

D is the approximate sales for week 5, or the result of adding 100 to the sales for week 6.

54. Correct response: **C**
(*Evaluate the reasonableness of a solution*)

One way to determine whether a solution is reasonable is to round the numbers in the problem to determine the appropriate number of digits in the solution. The theater sells approximately 12,000 tickets for approximately $30. $12,000 \times 30 = 360,000$, so the most reasonable solution will have 6 digits.

Incorrect choices:

A is not a reasonable solution because 3,856 is less than the number of tickets sold.

B would be a reasonable solution if the tickets cost $3 each instead of $32.

D is not a reasonable solution because it has too many digits.

Test ③ Answer Key

1. C	**12.** D	**23.** C	**34.** C	**45.** C
2. A	**13.** B	**24.** B	**35.** D	**46.** D
3. A	**14.** C	**25.** A	**36.** B	**47.** C
4. B	**15.** B	**26.** A	**37.** B	**48.** A
5. C	**16.** D	**27.** C	**38.** B	**49.** B
6. A	**17.** A	**28.** A	**39.** D	**50.** A
7. D	**18.** B	**29.** D	**40.** C	**51.** A
8. C	**19.** B	**30.** A	**41.** A	**52.** D
9. C	**20.** D	**31.** C	**42.** C	**53.** B
10. B	**21.** A	**32.** B	**43.** C	**54.** A
11. C	**22.** D	**33.** D	**44.** D	

Answer Key Explanations

1. Correct response: **C**
(*Compare and order whole numbers, fractions, and decimals*)

On this number line, the space between 0 and 1 is divided into 5 units, or fifths. Point F is located between the third and fourth hash marks, which represent $\frac{3}{5}$ and $\frac{4}{5}$ respectively. $\frac{3}{4}$ (or $\frac{15}{20}$) is between $\frac{3}{5}$ and $\frac{4}{5}$ ($\frac{12}{20}$ and $\frac{16}{20}$).

Incorrect choices:

A represents a computational error; $\frac{17}{20}$ is greater than $\frac{4}{5}$ (or $\frac{16}{20}$).

B represents a misinterpretation of the hash marks on the number line as 0.1, or $\frac{1}{10}$, instead of 0.2 for each mark.

D represents a computational error; $\frac{4}{10}$ is less than $\frac{3}{5}$ (or $\frac{12}{20}$).

2. Correct response: **A**
(*Compare, order, and use percents*)

The number of girls in Mr. McGarry's class is 36% of 25, or 9. The number of girls in Ms. Filipo's class is 55% of 20, or 11. The difference between 9 and 11 is 2.

Incorrect choices:

B is the difference between the total number of students in each class (25 − 20).

C is the number of girls in Mr. McGarry's class (0.36 × 25 = 9).

D is the number of girls in Ms. Filipo's class (0.55 × 20 = 11).

3. Correct response: **A**
(*Compare, order, and use integers*)

Tuesday's temperature was the only positive integer, and therefore the greatest.

3. (continued)
Incorrect choices:

B, **C**, and **D** represent misconceptions about integers. The temperatures on Wednesday and Thursday may appear higher than 1°C, but they are both negative integers. The temperature on Friday was 0°C, which is lower than 1°C.

4. Correct response: **B**
(*Identify and use place value*)
The hundredths place is two digits to the right of the decimal; in this case, it is a **4** (2,587.9**4**1).

Incorrect Choices:

A is in the thousandths place.

C is in the hundreds place.

D is in the tens place.

5. Correct response: **C**
(*Identify and describe prime and composite numbers, and prime factors*)
59 is a prime number and can't be divided evenly among 7 games.

Incorrect responses:

A, **B**, and **D** are all composite numbers and are all divisible by 7.

6. Correct response: **A**
(*Find factors and multiples*)
544 is divisible by 68 (544 ÷ 68 = 8), so each package could contain 8 pairs of socks.

Incorrect choices:

B, **C**, and **D** are not factors of 544, so none of them could be the number of packages the manager made.

7. Correct response: **D**
(*Use expanded notation, exponents, and scientific notation*)
The population of mice triples each year. That means that after the first year there will be 300 mice, or 100×3^1 mice. After the second year there will be 900 mice, or 100×3^2 mice. After 5 years, there will be 100×3^5 mice.

7. (continued)
Incorrect choices:

A does not take into account the original population of mice.

B would be a population growing by a power of 100 each year, not a power of 3.

C switches the number of years (5) with the power of growth (3).

8. Correct response: **C**
(*Use ratios to describe and compare two sets of data*)
The ratio of balls to strikes in each inning can be reduced to 3 to 2. For example, the ratio in the first inning was 6 to 4; $\frac{6}{4} = \frac{3}{2}$.

Incorrect choices:

A is the ratio of balls or strikes in the first inning to the number of balls or strikes in the second.

B is the ratio of balls or strikes in the second inning to the number of balls or strikes in the third.

D is the ratio of balls or strikes in the third inning to the number of balls or strikes in the fourth.

9. Correct response: **C**
(*Add, subtract, multiply, and divide whole numbers*)
The number of widgets produced in three days is 9,852 + 8,494 + 95, or 18,441.

Incorrect choices:

A is the sum of the first two numbers: 9,852 + 8,494.

B reflects an error in addition (the tens are not carried over to the next column).

D reflects an error in setting up the addition (the terms are not properly aligned by place value).

10. Correct response: **B**

(*Add, subtract, multiply, and divide fractions and mixed numbers*)

The amount of almonds she has left can be determined by subtraction: $20\frac{1}{2} - 15\frac{2}{3} = \frac{123}{6} - \frac{94}{6} = \frac{29}{6}$, or $4\frac{5}{6}$.

Incorrect choices:

A reflects an error in subtracting $\frac{123}{6} - \frac{94}{6}$, resulting in $\frac{28}{6}$.

C and **D** reflect errors in simplifying $\frac{29}{6}$.

11. Correct response: **C**

(*Add, subtract, multiply, and divide decimals*)

The number of square meters that Shakim can cover with both tarps is the sum of their areas, or $6.72 + 9.36 = 16.08$

Incorrect choices:

A reflects an error in adding 6.72 and 9.36 (not carrying the tenths to the next column).

B reflects an error in adding 6.72 and 9.36 (adding the decimal numbers 0.72 and 0.36 separately from the whole numbers 6 and 9).

D is the result of multiplying 6.72 by 9.36.

12. Correct response: **D**

(*Solve problems using ratios, rates, and proportions*)

The ratio of inches to miles on the map is 0.5 inches to 30 miles. If the cities are 2.5 inches apart on the map, the proportion to find the distance in real life will be $\frac{0.5}{30} = \frac{2.5}{x}$. Simplified, $x = 2.5 \times 60$, or 150 miles.

Incorrect choices:

A is the result of incorrect division ($\frac{0.5}{30} = \frac{1}{60}$, not $\frac{1}{15}$).

B is the result of dividing 30 by 0.5.

C is the result of multiplying 2.5 times 30.

13. Correct response: **B**

(*Solve problems involving integers*)

The change in temperature is $-25°C - (-10°C)$, or $-25°C + 10°C = -15°C$.

Incorrect choices:

A is the result of subtracting $-10°C - 25°C$.

C is the result of subtracting $-10°C - (-25°C) = 15°C$.

D is the result of adding $10°C + 25°C = 35°C$.

14. Correct response: **C**

(*Estimate and round using whole numbers and fractions*)

The weight of the white rice can be rounded to $1\frac{1}{2}$ lbs, and the weight of the brown rice can be rounded to $3\frac{1}{4}$ lbs. Together, they weigh about $4\frac{3}{4}$ lbs ($1\frac{1}{2}$ lbs + $3\frac{1}{4}$ lbs).

Incorrect choices:

A is the sum of 1 lb + 3 lbs; both numbers are rounded too low.

B is the sum of $1\frac{1}{4} + 3\frac{1}{4}$; the first number has been rounded incorrectly.

D is the sum of $1\frac{1}{2} + 3\frac{1}{2}$; the second number has been rounded incorrectly.

15. Correct response: **B**

(*Use order of operations to simplify whole-number expressions*)

The problem should be solved in the following order:

1. Simplify inside the parentheses:
$(6 + 4) \div 2 + 3 \times 6 = 10 \div 2 + 3 \times 6$

2. Divide and multiply, left to right:
$10 \div 2 + 3 \times 6 = 5 + 18$

3. Add: $5 + 18 = 23$

Incorrect choices:

A is the result of adding before dividing in step 2: $10 \div (2 + 3) \times 6$.

C is the result of ignoring the parentheses: $6 + (4 \div 2) + (3 \times 6)$.

D is the result of solving from left to right in sequence: $6 + 4 = 10$; $10 \div 2 = 5$; $5 + 3 = 8$; $8 \times 6 = 48$.

16. Correct response: **D**
(*Apply the properties of operations*)

Multiplication and division have an inverse relationship, so if $15 \times C = 840$, then $840 \div 15 = C$.

Incorrect choices:

A Addition cannot be substituted for multiplication.

B It sets up the inverse equation incorrectly.

C Addition does not have an inverse relationship with multiplication.

17. Correct response: **A**
(*Solve multi-step problems involving whole numbers and fractions*)

$\frac{3}{4}$ of the 180 students buy lunch: $180 \times \frac{3}{4} = 135$; $\frac{1}{3}$ of those students buy a sandwich: $135 \times \frac{1}{3} = 45$.

Incorrect choices:

B is the result of multiplying 180 times $\frac{1}{3}$.

C is the result of subtracting $(180 \times \frac{3}{4}) - (135 \times \frac{1}{3})$.

D is the result of multiplying 180 times $\frac{3}{4}$.

18. Correct response: **B**
(*Solve multi-step problems involving whole numbers and decimals*)

The cost of the two boxes of cereal is $2 \times \$3.29 = \$6.58$. When the price of the milk is added, the total cost is $\$6.58 + \$1.45 = \$8.03$. The coupon deducts $\$0.50$, so the total price Roberto pays is $\$8.03 - \$0.50 = \$7.53$.

Incorrect choices:

A accounts for only one box of cereal: $\$3.29 + \$1.45 - \$0.50$.

C reflects the total cost without the discount of $\$0.50$.

D reflects the total cost ($\$8.03$) plus the $\$0.50$, which should have been subtracted.

19. Correct response: **B**
(*Convert or estimate conversions of measures*)

If Andre doubles the recipe, he will need 6 cups $\times 2 = 12$ cups of milk. One quart $= 4$ cups, so 12 cups would be $12 \div 4 = 3$ quarts.

Incorrect choices:

A is the result of forgetting to double the recipe.

C is the result of forgetting to double the recipe and reversing the conversion (6×4 instead of $6 \div 4$).

D is the result of reversing the conversion (12×4 instead of $12 \div 4$).

20. Correct response: **D**
(*Estimate and find length and area*)

To find the area of the piece of paper, multiply the length by the width: 11 in. $\times$ 8.5 in. $= 93.5$ in.^{2}

Incorrect choices:

A is the sum of 11 in. $+$ 8.5 in.

B is the perimeter: $(8.5 \times 2) + (11 \times 2)$.

C is the area of the rectangle divided by 2 (as you would do for the area of a triangle).

21. Correct response: **A**
(*Estimate and find length and area*)

The area of the triangle is $\frac{1}{2}bh$, and $(\frac{1}{2})(4 \text{ m})(2.5 \text{ m}) = 5$ m^2.

Incorrect choices:

B is the sum of the two sides: $4 + 2.5$

C is the result of multiplying 4×2.5.

D is the result of multiplying 4×2.5 and doubling it instead of dividing by 2.

22. Correct response: **D**
(*Estimate and find weight/mass*)

The weight of the full bucket is the weight of the water (5 gallons $\times$ 8.3 lbs/gallon $= 41.5$ lbs) plus the weight of the bucket (0.6 lb) $= 42.1$ lbs.

22. (continued)
Incorrect choices:

A is the result of multiplying 5 times the weight of the bucket: 5×0.6 lb + 8.3 lbs.

B is the sum of the three numbers: 5 + 8.3 lbs + 0.6 lb.

C is the result of multiplying 5×8.3 lbs and subtracting 0.6 lb instead of adding.

23. Correct response: **C**
(*Identify and describe relationships among the radius, diameter, chord, center, and circumference of a circle*)

If point *A* is the center of the circle and point *B* is on the circle's edge, then the distance between them is the radius of the circle. This circle has a radius of 6 centimeters. The diameter is 2*r*, or 12 cm.

Incorrect choices:

A is the result of dividing the radius by 2 ($6 \div 2 = 3$) instead of multiplying.

B is the radius.

D is the result of multiplying the radius times π.

24. Correct response: **B**
(*Estimate and measure angles*)

∠*STU* is slightly greater than a right angle (90°), so the best estimate of its measure is 100°.

Incorrect choices:

A represents an angle that is slightly less than a right angle.

C represents an angle that is greater than ∠*STU*.

D represents an angle that is slightly larger than a straight angle.

25. Correct response: **A**
(*Classify acute, obtuse, and right angles and triangles*)

Since a square has four right angles, the largest angle of the shaded triangle is a right angle, making it a right triangle.

25. (continued)
Incorrect choices:

B The triangle has no obtuse angles.

C The triangle does not have three acute angles.

D The triangle does not have three equal sides; the diagonal of a square is greater than its side.

26. Correct response: **A**
(*Identify, classify, and describe plane figures*)

A diamond has four equal sides, whereas this shape has two sets of equal sides of differing lengths.

Incorrect choices:

B The figure is a rectangle because it has two sets of parallel sides and four right angles.

C The figure is a parallelogram because it has two sets of parallel sides.

D The figure is a quadrilateral because it has four sides.

27. Correct response: **C**
(*Determine congruence and similarity of segments, angles, and polygons*)

Δ*OLN* is congruent to Δ*MNL*, which means that their corresponding angles are congruent. ∠*OLN* corresponds to ∠*MNL*.

Incorrect choices:

A, B, and D represent angles that do not correspond to ∠*OLN*.

28. Correct response: **A**
(*Identify, classify, and describe solid figures*)
A cone's circular base is its only flat surface.

Incorrect choices:

B A cylinder has two flat circular bases.

C A triangular pyramid has four flat faces.

D A rectangular prism has six flat faces.

29. Correct response: **D**
(*Locate and name points on coordinate plane using ordered pairs*)
  The point that will create a rectangle with the three points on the grid will have the same y-value as point A and the same x-value as point C. Its location will be at (5, 9).

Incorrect choices:

A reverses the x- and y-values.

B represents the y-values of points B and A.

C represents the y-values of points A and B.

30. Correct response: **A**
(*Locate and name points on coordinate plane using ordered pairs*)
  Choice A shows a triangle with vertices at (2, 8), (5, 2), and (7, 4).

Incorrect choices:

B shows a triangle with vertices at points (8, 2), (5, 2), and (7, 4).

C shows a triangle with vertices at points (8, 2), (2, 5), and (4, 7).

D shows a triangle with vertices at points (8, 2), (5, 2), and (4, 7).

31. Correct response: **C**
(*Identify and describe points, lines, planes, and relationships among them*)
  The line made by the straw intersects the plane made by the lid of the cup where it passes through it.

Incorrect choices:

A The straw is not parallel to the lid; it intersects the lid.

B The straw is not perpendicular because it does not intersect the lid at a 90° angle.

D A line can intersect a plane.

32. Correct response: **B**
(*Transform figures in the coordinate plane*)
  Choice B shows the triangle rotated 180° about point A.

32. (continued)
 Incorrect choices:

A shows the triangle reflected over the line $y = 5$.

C shows the triangle reflected over the line $x = 4$.

D shows the triangle reflected over the line $x = 4$ and translated 2 units to the left.

33. Correct response: **D**
(*Solve problems involving volume and weight*)
  The volume of the sandbox equals length $\times$ width $\times$ depth: 15 ft $\times$ 9 ft $\times$ 2 ft = 270 ft³. If sand weighs 90 lbs/ft³, then the weight of 270 ft³ of sand is 270 ft³ $\times$ 90 lbs/ft³ = 24,300 lbs.

Incorrect choices:

A is the sum of the four numbers: 15 + 9 + 2 + 90.

B is the volume of the sandbox: 15 $\times$ 9 $\times$ 2.

C is the sum of the three measurements (15 + 9 + 2) multiplied by 90 lbs.

34. Correct response: **C**
(*Solve problems involving length, area, and time*)
  The area of the wall that needs to be painted is its length times its height, or 4.5 m $\times$ 2.5 m = 11.25 m². If it takes 15 minutes to paint 3 square meters, then the amount of time it takes to paint 1 square meter is 15 min/3 m² = 5 min/m². The total time required to paint the wall is its area (11.25 m²) multiplied by 5 min/m² = 56.25 minutes.

Incorrect choices:

A is the area of the wall (4.5 $\times$ 2.5) multiplied by $\frac{3}{15}$.

B is (4.5 + 2.5) $\times \frac{15}{3}$.

D is the area of the wall (4.5 $\times$ 2.5) multiplied by 15 minutes.

35. Correct response: **D**
(*Match 3-dimensional objects and their 2-dimensional representations*)
  The net shown in choice D can be folded to make a square pyramid.

35. (continued)

Incorrect choices:

A, **B**, and **C** cannot be folded to make square pyramids.

36. Correct response: **B**

(*Interpret data presented in a bar graph*)

Forty-six students chose comedy, which is more than twice the 22 students who chose science fiction.

Incorrect choices:

A The number of students who chose comedy (46) is less than the number of students who chose action (30) and drama (18) combined (48).

C The number of students who chose science fiction (22) is less than the total of the students who chose drama (18) and foreign (12) combined.

D The number of students who chose mystery (42) is less than the twice the number of students who chose action (30).

37. Correct response: **B**

(*Interpret data presented in a bar graph*)

Farrah counted about 44 bicycles in the afternoon, which is more than the number of trucks (28) plus the number of bicycles (12) she counted in the morning; 12 + 28 = 40.

Incorrect choices:

A Farrah counted more trucks in the morning (28) than in the afternoon (16).

C Farrah did not count more cars in the afternoon than all of the vehicles combined.

D The number of trucks Farrah counted in the morning (28) is less than the number of trucks (16) plus the number of bicycles (44) she counted in the afternoon.

38. Correct response: **B**

(*Interpret data in stem-and-leaf plots*)

The weight of the heaviest rat before the diet was 426 g. After the diet, 18 rats weighed more than 426 g.

Incorrect choices:

A is the number of rats weighing at least 430 grams.

C is the number of rats weighing at least 420 grams.

D is the total number of rats.

39. Correct response: **D**

(*Construct sample spaces using lists, charts, frequency tables, and tree diagrams*)

The sample space is the set of all possible outcomes of the experiment, or all possible pairs of color and heads or tails.

Incorrect choices:

A, **B**, and **C** represent misconceptions about constructing sample spaces.

40. Correct response: **C**

(*Find permutations and combinations*)

Since order matters when Carrie arranges the books, the answer should be the number of permutations. The number of permutations when repetition is not allowed (one book cannot be placed first and second) is $n!$; in this case, $n = 4$ and $4! = 4 \times 3 \times 2 \times 1 = 24$.

Incorrect choices:

A is $4 + 4$.

B is 4×4 or $4 + 4 + 4 + 4$.

D is $4 \times 4 \times 4 \times 4$.

41. Correct response: **A**

(*Find probabilities*)

There are 8 sections on the spinner, and 3 of the 8 sections will allow a player to move more than 5 spaces (6, 7, or 8). The probability that the arrow will land on one of those sections is $\frac{3}{8}$.

41. (continued)

Incorrect choices:

B is the probability that a player will move at least 5 spaces.

C is the number 5 over the total number of sections (8).

D is the number of successful spins (3) over the number of unsuccessful spins (5).

42. Correct response: **C**
(*Determine and compare experimental and theoretical probabilities for simple and compound events, independent and dependent events*)

The probability of choosing a girl's name first is $\frac{9}{15}$. After that name is removed, there are only 14 names in the hat, and 6 are boys' names. The probability of choosing a boy's name second is $\frac{6}{14}$. The probability of choosing a girl's name first and a boy's name second is $\frac{9}{15} \times \frac{6}{14} = \frac{54}{210}$, or $\frac{9}{35}$.

Incorrect choices:

A is the sum of $\frac{9}{15} + \frac{6}{15}$.

B is the product of $\frac{9}{15} \times \frac{6}{15}$.

D is the sum of $\frac{9}{15} + \frac{6}{14}$.

43. Correct response: **C**
(*Determine and describe the mean, median, mode, and range of data*)

To find the median, put all of the numbers in order and find the middle value. Since there are 20 numbers, there are two middle values (8 and 9). The mean of these numbers is the median. $(8 + 9) \div 2 = 8.5$.

Incorrect choices:

A is the mode of the data.

B is the 10th value in order, mistaken for the median.

D is the mean of the data.

44. Correct response: **D**
(*Determine and describe the mean, median, mode, and range of data*)

To find the mean, add all of the rainfall values together (156) and divide by the number of months (6): $156 \div 6 = 26$.

44. (continued)

Incorrect choices:

A is the range of the data $(34 - 18)$.

B is the 3rd number in the chart, mistaken for the mean.

C is the median of the data.

45. Correct response: **C**
(*Collect, organize, display, and interpret data to solve problems*)

A line graph is the best way for Jerome to display how the amount of money has changed over time.

Incorrect choices:

A is a type of display that is good for showing percentages, or parts of a whole.

B and **D** are types of display that are good for organizing data to show trends, median, and mode.

46. Correct response: **D**
(*Identify, describe, and extend numerical patterns*)

Each week, the number of lily pads grows by 30. The expression that describes the number of lily pads on the pond in relation to week n is $30n + 2$. In week 7, the number of lily pads on the pond will be $30(7) + 2 = 212$.

Incorrect choices:

A is the number of lily pads in week 5.

B is the number of lily pads in week 6.

C represents an error in arithmetic.

47. Correct response: **C**
(*Interpret, write, and simplify algebraic expressions*)

The total amount of money in Manuel's account can be found by adding $82 + $25, plus the amount earned each day ($0.02) times the number of days (n), or $0.02n.

47. (continued)

Incorrect choices:

A does not account for the number of days.

B adds the interest for only one day ($0.02) to the number of days (*n*).

D multiplies the amount of money in the account times the number of days.

48. Correct response: **A**

(*Apply basic properties and order of operations with algebraic expressions*)

Using the associative property, $(5 + x) + x = 5 + (x + x)$, or $5 + 2x$. Using the distributive property, $3(x + 4) = 3x + 12$. The whole expression is equivalent to $\dfrac{5 + 2x}{3x + 12}$.

Incorrect choices:

B reflects a misunderstanding of the distributive property, resulting in $3x + 4$.

C reflects a misunderstanding of the distributive property and an error in adding $(5 + x) + x$.

D reflects an error in multiplying $(5 + x) + x$ instead of adding.

49. Correct response: **B**

(*Model, represent, and solve mathematical relationships with tables, graphs, and rules using words or symbols*)

All of the values in the input-output table in choice B fit the rule of $3x - 1$: $3(4) - 1 = 11$; $3(7) - 1 = 20$; $3(9) - 1 = 26$

Incorrect choices:

A shows the results for input *n* if the output will be $3n + 1$.

C switches the input and output values; for example, $3(2) - 1 = 5$.

D switches the input and output values and adds 1 instead of subtracting 1; for example, $3(1) + 1 = 4$.

50. Correct response: **A**

(*Solve one-step and two-step linear equations*)

To solve for *r*, divide both sides by 6:

$$\frac{6r}{6} = \frac{18}{6}$$

$$r = 3$$

Incorrect choices:

B is the result of subtracting $18 - 6$.

C is the result of adding $18 + 6$.

D is the result of multiplying 18×6.

51. Correct response: **A**

(*Solve simple one-step and two-step inequalities*)

To solve the inequality, first subtract 2,500 from each side:

$$2,500 + 20b - 2,500 < 5,000 - 2,500$$

$$20b < 2,500$$

Then divide each side by 20 to get the answer: $b < 125$. The driver can carry any number of boxes less than 125.

Incorrect choices:

B flips the inequality sign, making the number of boxes greater than 125.

C is the result of adding 2,500 to 5,000.

D is the result of adding 2,500 to 5,000 and flipping the inequality sign.

52. Correct response: **D**

(*Represent linear functions using tables, equations, and graphs*)

The line shown in the graph has a slope of 3 and a *y*-intercept of 6, so its equation is $y = 3x + 6$.

Incorrect choices:

A, **B**, and **C** all represent misconceptions about the relationship between the graph and its linear equation.

53. Correct response: **B**

(*Make conjectures, predictions, and generalizations from patterns, data, or examples*)

The average number of jars sold per day after advertising in the newspaper is about $2\frac{1}{2}$, or 2.5, times greater than the average number of jars sold per day before any advertising. For example, ginger peach jam sold 20 jars per day before advertising and 50 jars afterward ($2.5 \times 20 = 50$). The new jam sells 12 jars per day before advertising and will likely sell about 30 jars ($2.5 \times 12 = 30$) afterward.

Incorrect responses:

A is a good prediction of sales after advertising in the store (approximately twice as many jars as before advertising).

C estimates that sales will triple ($3 \times 12 = 36$).

D estimates that sales will quadruple ($4 \times 12 = 48$).

54. Correct response: **A**

(*Evaluate the reasonableness of a solution*)

The club raised just under half of the money it hoped to make, so the number of brownies sold on the second day should be slightly larger than the number sold on the first day. If they sold 98 on the first day, then they have to sell just over 100 on the second day (107 brownies would result in earnings of $170.13, for a total of $325.95.), so 105 is the most reasonable estimate.

Incorrect choices:

B is just under the number of brownies sold on the first day and would result in less than $325.

C and **D** are considerably less than the number of brownies that would need to be sold.

Standardized Test Tutor: Math   Grade 6

Student Scoring Chart

Student Name _____

Teacher Name _____

Test 1	Item Numbers	Number Correct/Total	Percent (%)
Number and Number Sense	1–8	/8	
Operations	9–18	/10	
Measurement and Geometry	19–36	/18	
Statistics and Probability	37–45	/9	
Patterns, Relations, and Algebra	46–54	/9	
Total	**1–54**	**/54**	

Test 1	Item Numbers	Number Correct/Total	Percent (%)
Number and Number Sense	1–8	/8	
Operations	9–18	/10	
Measurement and Geometry	19–35	/17	
Statistics and Probability	36–45	/10	
Patterns, Relations, and Algebra	46–54	/9	
Total	**1–54**	**/54**	

Test 1	Item Numbers	Number Correct/Total	Percent (%)
Number and Number Sense	1–8	/8	
Operations	9–18	/10	
Measurement and Geometry	19–35	/17	
Statistics and Probability	36–45	/10	
Patterns, Relations, and Algebra	46–54	/9	
Total	**1–54**	**/54**	

Comments/Notes:_____

_____

Standardized Test Tutor: Math   Grade ⑥

Classroom Scoring Chart

Teacher Name _____

Student Name	Test 1	Test 2	Test 3